A Walk with
APHRODITE

Peter Breakwell

KYRIAKOU BOOKS

A **KYRIAKOU** BOOK

First published 1998 - paperback edition
by K.P.Kyriakou (books - stationery) Ltd
P. O.Box 159 Limassol. Cyprus
✆ 05-747555 Fax. 05-371706

Distributed by **KYRIAKOU BOOKSHOPS**

ISBN 9963-571-59-X

CONTENTS

DEDICATION

This book is a journey of love
for my wife
Joanna

ACKNOWLEDGEMENTS

I sincerely wish to thank all those I was fortunate enough to meet, who gave food and shelter to a total stranger, for without their infinate kindness and generosity my journey would never have been completed.

I am grateful to Dorathy Dow, Bett and Jim Scott and Dr. Phylactis from the Paphos hospital's charity, who helped and supported me, throughout. Moreover, the publishers and myself wish to thank Alan Breakwell, by brother, for accepting the commissioned work of illustrations that appear in this book.

CHAPTER 1

APHRODITE

So varied is the reference to Aphrodite in ancient text, that the Greek writers and poets who preserved her fame in the Classical period inadvertently caused much confusion. There can be little doubt, however, that for more than three thousand years the passionate images of Aphrodite have prevailed. For whether you believe in legend or not, one cannot ignore the enchantment she has weaved across this region. Aphrodite is still the most endearing feature of Cyprus' long and turbulent history.

Like every romantic before me, I had come to this tranquil place trying to determine her mysterious origin. Here, it was said, in a small rock-strewn bay known as Petra tou Romiou... the Goddess of Love was borne from the sea.

The April sun felt warm and comforting, as did the rock I sat upon, its surface worn to a crescent by a million believers who had rested here... or was this, too, the magic of the sea? For many times during a storm, when breakers strike this beach at a certain angle, a receding wave will encounter the incoming swell and launch a waterspout several metres high. As it falls, the cascading water appears as a human figure with flowing hair and outstretched arms.

There was no storm that morning - the ocean barely whispered at my feet. But when you are alone in this bay it is not easy to distinguish illusion from reality. Even as you watch the silent sea... there seems an unmistakable presence.

Graphic illustrations of Aphrodite's birth from the ocean are numerous, and perhaps the most admired are featured on the base of the statue of Zeus at Olympia, or the relief on the Ludovisi throne in Rome. But probably her finest portrayal of all is Botticelli's masterpiece: 'The Birth of Venus'.

A number of Renaissance artists were intrigued by the Romans and Ancient Greeks, yet Sandro Botticelli's painting in the mid-sixteenth century was revolutionary for its time. Presenting Venus as a marble-like Roman statue, softened by her long golden hair, his mastery symbolized all the poetic imagery of the Classical writers. Her origin, explained Hesiod, being in her very name 'aphro' - meaning foam. To the Greeks, therefore, she is always known as Aphrodite; it was the Romans who named her Venus.

I sat recalling the words of a friendly poet from Koili, my adopted village in Paphos... 'You may well feel her presence in the scent of the earth, or from the kiss of the west wind,' he said. 'She can be seen in mid-April. Look for her in the bay, my friend, for she comes with the first warmth of the year.' The old man's eyes had twinkled. 'Here,' he smiled. 'Take this rose and cast it into the sea, for this is the flower sacred to her birth - its beauty and fragrance is the symbol of love.'

Indeed, my visit coincided with the time of year: the day

was warm, and Zephyr's west wind lent a gentle ripple to the waves. But even though Aphrodite had vanished with the gods, a world of dreams still lingered on. It was not difficult to imagine her elegant beauty alighting from a scallop shell, or to hear the laughter of her maidens whenever the sea caressed this pebbled shore. The tranquillity of it all filled me with an inner calm: a resolve that I certainly needed for the arduous journey I was about to undertake. In twenty-four hours I would begin to follow her imaginary footsteps from the sea. Here, proclaim the ancients, where limestone cliffs rise into an endless sky... is where it all began.

My reverie was disturbed by the day's first coach load of tourists - it was time to go. The rose had returned unbroken to the beach, its blood-red petals glistening in the sun. I presented it to the first young lady I met: she was oriental - more of a tiny Madam Butterfly than Aphrodite, but her smile was no less beautiful.

It was ten o'clock when I returned to Kato Paphos. After parking my car near the harbour, I spent the next few hours visiting all the gift shops, restaurants and hotels that I could. It would be difficult asking people to pledge their hard earned money to a total stranger, but armed with a clip board and an official looking letter I had prepared in England, I set off in an optimistic mood.

The letter outlined a charitable purpose to my impending walk, with its beneficiary as Paphos General Hospital. It also stated my intention to visit more than a hundred villages and towns throughout the district of Paphos. A solitary journey on foot that would traverse seven hundred kilometres of the region's most formidable and isolated terrain.

In reply, I received a variety of friendly remarks and gestures: a few shook their heads in disbelief, others smiled, knowingly. But such is the generosity of the Cypriots to a genuine cause that no-one refused to support me. In three hours I had promises of almost six hundred pounds. Not a king's ransom by any means, but it was an encouraging start that would help Dorathy, the charity organizer I was due to meet later that afternoon. She was kind enough on behalf of 'Plentyniners' - the hospital's charity - to take on board the logistics of the walk while I was in England. Our contact had been by letter and telephone, and although this was not the ideal situation, she achieved everything possible on my behalf. Following a light meal near the harbour, I left the boats to sigh and creak on its swell and drove out to Chlorakas.

I was immediately impressed by Dorathy's enthusiasm. No-one could have wished for a better person to run the show. A meeting had been planned at the hospital, closely followed by a live interview with the local radio. The next morning, I was informed, both radio and television crews would be waiting for me at Petra tou Romiou before the walk began.

My arrival at the hospital was greeted with warmth and appreciation from doctors and nurses, alike. Mr Phylactis Constantinides, Director of the Surgical and Endoscopy Unit, welcomed me on behalf of his staff, and we chatted over coffee like old friends. Phylactis was also patron of the fund raising group, and explained the desperate need of providing specialized equipment for the hospital's Gynaecology Department.

Paphos General Hospital had been inaugurated in March 1992 by George Vasiliou, the island's President at that

Petra tou Romiou or Petra tou Digeni

time. It was built by the people of Paphos with American finance, together with grants from the Resettlement Fund of the Council of Europe. This splendid building was re-sited from the old hospital which had cost eight hundred pounds to build in 1909. This money being funded by private enterprise, with the government contributing a detached dispensary. The hospital held just twenty-two beds and was managed by a Board, headed by a Commissioner.

Old or new, hospitals are not a favourite place of mine... except as a visitor. Little did I realize when I said my good-byes, that nine days later I would be returning as a patient! I also found the prospect of giving a live radio interview unnerving. But well supported by Dorathy and Bett, another member of the charity team, I struggled through for an hour as a guest of Tony Patal in his five o'clock show on Radio Paphos. Tony had suffered serious injuries in a road accident and, apparently saved by the surgical skills of Doctor Phylactis, now supported the charity whenever possible. He was a likeable fellow; it was a pity my nervousness detracted from his fine choice of records.

Next morning, I sat on the patio of my house in Koili village watching the sun rise over the Troodos mountains. The sky, coloured with pastel shades of red and orange, glimmered as though the embers of an enormous fire lay dying in the forests beyond. The whole panorama from Mount Olympus to the far western slopes of Tilliria reflected a wonderful serenity. An early mist shrouded the vineyards below the cottage, creating its own ghostly image of a lake swirling into the northern valley. Yet in a few hours, even distant peaks would reveal their rugged features, and the greenery of Paphos forest would unfold some twenty-five kilometres away. After drinking my second mug of hot tea, I checked my backpack one more time before leaving the village.

No more than a dozen people awaited my arrival at Petra tou Romiou, but I felt nervously excited by their presence. Being interviewed by radio and television crews is a daunting experience, however, so I was relieved when at last the time came for handshakes and best wishes to send me on my way. Having secured my backpack to the tension marks on its straps, I set off on a unique journey into the heart of Aphrodite's realm.

A breeze was freshening the sea and white-capped waves danced between the enormous rocks down in the bay. Cast there, it was said, by Digenis, legendary hero of Medieval Byzantinium, who hurled them at the Saracens to protect his queen in mythical sea battles. They lie scattered along this coastline, thrown by a warrior whose fingerprints are visibly etched into the stone. Yet it seems even heroes are doomed. For in Cypriot song he was conquered by Charon, the aged ferryman who conveyed the spirits of the dead to Hades. They wrestled for three days - then, to overcome Digenis' incredible strength Charon transformed himself into an eagle, and driving his talons into the warrior's skull... plucked out his soul.

Heading west along the main Paphos/Limassol highway, I hoped my presence would not stir the wrath of Digenis, and henceforth, all ferrymen and eagles had my utmost respect... The traffic was heavy, thundering past in an endless stream of pollution. It was a relief when I could turn away from the diesel fumes and climb northwards across Chapotami.

The area, named after its river, was a strange mixture of wild terrain, tarmac roads and paved footpaths. A few houses were visible, and apparently a golf course had been planned on the site. But the government was clearly opposed to water resources from the nearby Asprokremos Dam being used for anything other than domestic and agricultural means. It was estimated that because of the island's long hot summers an eighteen-hole golf course would use two million cubic tonnes of water each year. The proposition to plan such a project hardly seemed viable. Besides this, I had been warned the whole promontory was an infamous habitat for snakes! It seemed I was walking through a developer's worst nightmare. The great injustice of it all was the fact that somewhere under my feet lay the remains of a road built by the Romans. In the first century it stretched from the ancient city of Kourion, a few kilometres east, to Paphos in the west, and had been used through the Middle Ages into modern times.

The track from Chapotami ended at the top of a deep gorge. There was no pathway down, and while carefully zigzagging my way between the rocks I disturbed a blunt-nosed viper. This is the most deadly of the few poisonous snakes in Cyprus. The scrub was waist high in places, but fortunately it lay sunning itself in a small clearing. I froze like a statue, watching it slither away into the undergrowth. Snakes have an acute sense of smell, and whenever they become aware of approaching humans they tend to move away. Nevertheless, I stood rooted to the spot.

During the time I had lived in Paphos I was privileged enough to meet Hans-Joerg Wiedl, an intrepid Austrian who became affectionately known to the Cypriots as

'Snake George'. He had been trying since 1990 to educate, or even modify, their ancient belief of all creatures that slithered on the ground being a mortal threat. His advice to me was crucial because of travelling alone, but in remote areas like this it proved difficult to follow. Here, for example, I could not avoid the high grass. But I was particularly cautious regarding pools of water near bushes, as these too, are favourite spots for the viper.

Snakes, I learned, adapt their blood temperature to their surroundings: moving slowly in the cool morning air due to a low body warmth, but once aroused by the sun they become active. A more likely time to encounter a snake is towards evening when the earth has stored its heat for the day. In doing so, I should adopt safe and sensible procedures.

I was thankful this was not the eighteenth century, when the Cyprus asp (vipera mauritanica) was reputed to grow to almost two metres in length and up to thirty-eight centimetres in diameter. With a bite so quick and light it was hardly felt... but its poison was deadly. The infected area became swollen, its victim grew pale and then livid as the poison clogged his veins. Within a few hours - crippled with lethargy, nausea and depression - he would begin to shiver and suffer convulsions. Then as blood circulation congealed, death occurred. Naturally, I decided to give any snake a very wide berth!

On top of a ridge on the far side of the gorge I could see the village of Kouklia. It lay a fair distance south-west of the route I had chosen - a good sign, at least, that my compass was working well. In less than two hours I had reached the road to Archimandrita, and finding the welcome shade of a citrus grove, decided to rest. I removed my heavy pack and sat under the umbrella of an orange tree nibbling chocolate. Looking around I could see the orchard was still a mass of fruit, much of it left to rot under the trees. So rescuing two juicy oranges from the branches above, I satisfied both hunger and thirst before moving out again into the sun.

Along the roadside, splashes of white and yellow anthemis stirred in a cooling breeze. I wandered between fields of ripening corn, speckled with blood-red poppies... yet all too soon the way lost its affection, twisting and turning into a long intimidating climb. I had to submit near its peak, collapsing in a heap at the roadside. Below was a deep ravine, and over the hazy landscape beyond I could see a sprinkling of villages. Earlier, I had passed a range of corrugated buildings where goats loudly complained to the two black-clothed women herding them into the sheds. A whiff of their alternative protests now hit me on the breeze... it was time to reach for my handkerchief and move on.

A signpost signalled eight kilometres to Pano Archimandrita - but I wasn't counting, for I looked upon this as a distraction. Negative thoughts are a hazard. The discomfort of blistering feet; straps eating into your shoulders; the annoyance of a belt being too tight - too loose; or a creaking backpack that begins to fray your nerves when you're tired and thirsty... Any one of these creates mental havoc for a lone walker. But I had been meticulous with my pack to ensure the right balance. Straps and belt tensions were pre-marked so that nothing flapped around or squeaked. I was pleased to have taken the time - it certainly avoided unnecessary hassle in the formidable days ahead.

Two pick-up trucks had already stopped to offer me a lift along this stretch, the third awoke me with its screeching brakes. Lured by the shade and sweet aroma of the trees, I lay dozing on a bed of pine needles at the roadside when the startled driver saw me. I caught the words... *'o yiatros'* as he peered anxiously at my spread-eagled form. So I had to stand brushing the dust from my trousers before I convinced him that I was uninjured. His old, but still handsome features, creased with laughter when I explained that I was walking across Paphos.

'Walk?' he roared. 'Panagia!... Only the crazy English walk in this sun.' He meant no insult, his eyes stared more in admiration when he shook my hand. *'Kalo taxidi,'* he smiled, wishing me well as he drove away towards Kouklia.

The valley on my left deepened, its wilderness now transformed into a sprawling mosaic of green pastures and vineyards. At last I was descending. My road swept me into this chasm where I could see the houses of Archimandrita shimmering on a northern ridge. Yet another climb ahead... but with the promise of an ice-cold beer rewarding the effort, a spring returned to my stride.

Many villages in Paphos have particular attractions for the traveller. It may be a historic building; some artistic interest; an archaeological site; or perhaps the charismatic nature of the villagers themselves. Archimandrita, a sign told me, held the remains of three hundred and eighteen saints in a tomb known as the hermitage of Agioi Pateres. An arrow pointed the way - but my empty stomach insisted that human remains were no substitute for food. I trudged on into the village.

The coffee-shop was small but ample for the villagers, Neophytos informed me. 'There are only seventy people here now,' he sighed. He was a big man, but his movements were quick and nimble as he arranged me space at a solitary table.

'When I was a boy,' he continued, 'the village was four hundred strong. But all the young one's have left now. Gone for...' His voice trailed away and he ran a bony finger across his throat. 'When we die, Archimandrita finish,' he said... 'All over! You understand?'

I sipped my beer, nodding sympathetically. The ham sandwiches I had unpacked tasted good. Neophytos watched me, his sunburned hands gently rolling a string of worry-beads between his fingers. 'A present from Romania,' he beamed. Then, nodding towards my backpack... 'How much did you pay for that?'

'What? Do you mean everything?'

He lit up his second cigarette since my appearance and, as if suddenly tiring of conversation, returned to his chair by the doorway without waiting for an answer. This apparent rudeness was not meant to offend me; it's a harmless gesture I had witnessed many times before. In the coffee-shops men will leave in mid-conversation without any discernible reason - they just up and go in a muted farewell. I continued eating in silence.

The room was a typical *cafenion*: strewn with hard rickety chairs and two fridges which held beer and pop. This one also contained an old cabinet filled with medicines, batteries, boot polish and bottled spirits... all gathering dust. There was a chipped sink beside a single gas hob, where Neophytos now stood brewing his Greek coffee. My table was covered by a plastic cloth, its fading pattern riddled with cigarette burns. And behind me, carrier bags filled with crisps hung on rusting nails. While flies buzzed around the crumbs of my sandwich I tried to determine what draped along the rafters.

'Plastic!' Neophytos had followed my gaze. 'Just old sheets of plastic... Keeps out the winter rain,' he chuckled.

I finished my beer and joined him on the step for a while before making my way back to the chapel tomb.

At the top of the hill a vast panorama unfolded my journey from the sea. In the eastern valley once flowed the Chapotami river, its southern reaches revealing a Roman milestone, dated from the proconsulate of Audius Bassus. I imagined the human remains I was about to see would come from a more brutal era... The tomb was not a sight for the faint hearted.

It was situated at the base of a stairway in a neat courtyard. A stone cross marked the chapel entrance, and nearby, a sign in Greek forbid me to light wax tapers or candles inside. I opened the door, and it moaned and creaked as I entered the musty darkness of a small cave.

From the open doorway a shaft of light revealed a metal grill in the rock wall... through which, stared the empty sockets of two shiny skulls. As my eyes grew accustomed to the semi-darkness I observed a large niche behind the bars. Inside, countless human bones and skulls filled the tomb. It was a small and eerie graveyard for the saints, who were alleged to have been slaughtered by a band of savages arriving in Paphos after fleeing persecution in Syria. I wondered if the weird-looking effigies behind the chapel door might be significant to those heathens and their terrible sins?

The day's heat was fading as I returned to the village. Neophytos had moved his chair and sat alone in the sun. I retrieved my pack, thanking him for his company.

'One day soon you must come back,' he smiled... 'before all of Archimandrita turns to bones!' He wished me luck and pointed the way to my next village.

Mousere was north-east towards the Limassol boundary - a steady climb that turned the cultured landscape into harsh scrub land again. The tarmac road became a dusty limestone track, and after a few kilometres I stopped to consult my maps.

The locality was a dumping ground for cookers, fridges, bikes and general household rubbish. A needless sight - not uncommon in deserted areas. The sun-bleached skull of a goat surveyed this atrocity from the fork of a carob tree. I trudged on in dismay.

My intention was to stay the night at a monastery north-west of this point, which meant back-tracking from Mousere two kilometres in order to resume my route. This I did in a hurry as the light was beginning to wane, and Mousere had nothing to offer but a few deserted houses and an overgrown cemetery.

The track to the monastery deteriorated, but I made good progress down the wooded slopes. Birds cooed and twittered through the pines signalling their time to roost, while below, a setting sun had left the valley dark and still. Soon I had reached the Aphorismenos Plain, and blackening the northern skies towered the Troodos mountains. I had no more than an hour to find the monastery before someone turned out the light completely.

Agios Savvas tis Karonas was a post-Byzantine monastery. Its church had been rebuilt at the start of the sixteenth century and restored again some two hundred years later. The stonework dependencies of both church and monastery were admirable, and recent reports on renovation work there had raised my hopes for some form of shelter. I arrived to find a different story.

Clambering through the undergrowth I eventually reached a semicircle of stone steps. Under a Gothic arch its narrow doors were locked and bolted. I searched around, failing to find even a suitable outbuilding to shelter in. Now forced to abandon my original plan, I retraced my steps to the track. Sadly, to sleep under the protective eyes of its icons was not to be. As nightfall wrapped itself around me, a chill wind murmured through the valley. I headed for the Diarizos river.

On its far western slopes the beams of car headlights raked the mountain roads, and suddenly the land became void of trees. I had no choice but to stop at the most convenient place I could find to pitch a tent. Off loading my backpack, I quickly removed small rocks and stones from the ground to make a suitable clearing.

The tent had been fun to erect in the back garden at home... but that was with help and in broad daylight! Now, alone in the darkness with no experience whatsoever in the complexities of camping, I attempted to salvage a bed for the night. On your knees by torch light was not the recommended method in the booklet, but I persevered, and following its first total collapse around my ears, I eventually scrambled inside. Eight-thirty, however, was not my normal idea of an early night...

CHAPTER 2

REFLECTIONS

Apart from an aching shin I felt in good shape. My first ten hours had revealed some important 'do's and don'ts': I must always ensure that I check nothing is left behind whenever I rest; much to my dismay, stopping at the goat-skull tree had cost me a sun-hat. Also, I certainly needed to pace myself better, particularly when walking in the hot sun. With my inferior lung capacity I had attempted too much at times, causing exhaustion, and ultimately, a loss of time. Still, I was pleased to have reached the Diarizos valley; albeit, the night was young and I was perched on a downward tilt, but the day's effort seemed a reasonable achievement for an ageing novice.

My dome tent was roomy enough, and at one and a half kilos, the lightest I could find anywhere in my intended price range. Now and again the wind would sweep the valley floor, but the tent-pegs held firm in the rocky earth so I was happy to finish my remaining sandwiches for supper.

The previous months had not been as satisfying. Trying to promote my ideas for the walk in Cyprus proved frustrating. During a visit to the island in mid-October, I had approached the Mayor of Paphos and his Cultural and

Public Relations Officer regarding the correct procedures in Cyprus for staging such an event. The final analysis was threefold: first of all, it was paramount that I obtained permission from the government's Health Minister; secondly, a letter of acceptance from the District Officer of Paphos; and finally, I would need a recognized charity or sponsor on the island to organize things on my behalf.

Because of the journey's great distance and time factor, however, I was also advised that the project would be impractical. A solitary walker could never have the desired impact, or indeed, carry facilities to advertise or collect donations over such a long period of time. Undeterred, I thanked them for the names and addresses of relevant contacts and returned to England.

There was no easy solution. After a dozen letters to shipping and air lines, banks, building contractors, estate agents and wineries, no sponsorship was forthcoming. My only success being a kind donation from Leptos Estates - the island's renowned property developers - and an encouraging letter from Dorathy Dow, informing me that a hospital's charity in Paphos would be delighted to help me out. This proved to be a turning point, which led to another open door when I received acknowledgement from Paphos' District Officer. Meanwhile, a simple idea overcame the problem of collecting money through the towns and villages along the way.

After several days of planning I devised the most systematic route possible, and again wrote to the District Officer, Mr Giorgallides, requesting his assistance. Enclosing a copy of my suggested route and dates of arrival, therein, meant that people would be aware of my coming, and hopefully, their donations made readily available to me from the village head - or *mukhtar*. For this purpose, I politely suggested a letter of authority from the District Officer notifying all *mukhtars* within his region of the appropriate dates. Eventually, this was agreed.

Through further correspondence with the charity, I reiterated my intentions that all proceeds from the walk would be donated to their cause, the Paphos General Hospital. Obtaining permission from the government's Health Minister, however, remained inconclusive. An official letter - promised in February - never materialized, and the walk commenced with only his verbal acknowledgement. Administration, I found, was not one of the island's most popular conformities.

The maps I required for my journey were, it seemed, unavailable even at the larger stockists in London, so during my stay in October I visited the Department of Lands and Surveys in Nicosia. I decided upon their Cadastral Survey Maps in the K717 Series - with a scale of 1 : 50,000 - and found that five were necessary to cover the Paphos district. They were notably coloured and shaded, with fine detail of tracks and pathways, upon which I would have to rely in order to tackle the vast expanse of the region. Each map contained a glossary and informative sections that listed the whole topography of the area. They were ideal for my requirements.

In the initial planning stages I devised and rejected several alternatives before deciding on my eventual route. It was made as compact and conservative as possible. Yet with more than one hundred villages to negotiate it was impossible not to backtrack at times; ultimately, however, the distance involved proved negligible. From Petra tou Romiou to Kannaviou, my journey would undertake a series of punishing climbs across the region's three most distinctive valleys before reaching the north-western splendours of Chrysokhou Bay. But for now, spending my first night on the eastern banks of the Diarizos river was proving a somewhat uncomfortable experience.

In my haste to erect the tent I had left too many stones which sprouted like spiked mushrooms whenever I moved. I lay awake for hours listening to the strange whimpers and flutterings in the valley. When sleep came it was broken abruptly by the sound of something scratching nearby. I fumbled in the darkness for my torch, and slowly unzipping the tent flaps, crawled outside.

In the torchlight a dog scampered away towards the monastery disturbing an owl that screeched over my head like a startled witch. There was no peace of mind after this. I cat-napped until dawn then walked down to the river, washing and shaving in its icy waters. Refreshed by the warm fingers of sunlight caressing the valley, I changed into a clean shirt, carefully packed my tent and returned to the river.

I headed north-east along its banks, but after a while the dense undergrowth forced me to wade across several times before I saw Prastio. Somewhere... the morning dew moistened a citrus grove, and orange blossom filled the air with a fragrance that only Aphrodite could stir. A kingfisher skimmed the waters at my feet, its colours flashing in the dappled sunlight that filtered through the trees. Then just as swiftly, nature seemed to die as I reached the empty shell of a village.

Prastio was no more than a few heaps of stone littering a hillside. I could not determine its late fifteenth century church, the only visible place of worship was where I stood near the river. Agios Ilias was a church cut into a rocky outcrop, but this too, appeared as a crumbling nonentity. There were no signs of reverence, merely a cross high in the rocks above its entrance. I avoided this rugged incline, moving on to find a narrow path that climbed sharply to the main road.

The nagging pain in my shin returned, and on the way to Kidasi I stopped to rest in a leafy glade. Perched on the parapet of a bridge above the river, I pondered over such an early dilemma. There was no sign of an injury; aches and pains in a few other places where the stony mattress had skewered me the previous night, but this was more serious. I rubbed in some ointment from my medical kit and resumed at a slower pace, hoping the problem would wear off.

In the weeks before my arrival I had walked on several occasions carrying a full pack; it hardly seemed possible my legs were cracking up so soon? True, I was a novice, but a well prepared one... or so I assumed. Nevertheless, I was still breaking the golden rule of walkers going it alone; for even though my charity friends knew my route each day they had no trace of me in the wilderness. Apart from the island's military bases there were no rescue services to speak of.

As I journeyed on my thoughts focused on a more positive trait: testing my memory banks on the gear I carried was a trivial, but effective pastime. Here is my list of essentials, remembered.

2	sun hats	45 litre backpack
	sunglasses*	drinking flask
3	tee-shirts*	torch
	a sweater	army knife
2	pairs of cotton trousers*	compass
	shorts	whistle
2	pairs of underpants	waterproofs
5	pairs of cotton socks	tent
	trainers	ground mat
2	handkerchiefs	camera & film
	pyjamas	maps
	reading glasses	note pads & pens
	walking boots & spare laces*	sleeping bag

Toiletries & Medical kit

toothbrush & paste	TCP ointment
comb	second skin
mirror	insect repellent
razor	E45 cream
soap	plasters
towel	bandages
sun lotion	embrocation
toilet roll	glucose tablets

* denotes the following information:

'Sunglasses': although essential in the bright sunshine, my journey was planned so that I followed an east to west route. This meant on the majority of occasions the fierce sun would be on my back - not blurring my vision.

'Tee-shirts': a fresh shirt was in my pack, one worn during the day, the third being draped around my neck to prevent sunburn. They were kindly laundered by my charity team along the way.

'Cotton trousers': these were worn in preference to shorts. A sensible choice considering the rough terrain I had already experienced. Sunburned legs would only add unnecessary discomfort.

'Walking boots': in hindsight, they could not be faulted, and proved the most important purchase I ever made.

Whilst in England, I had watched the television series of Ffyona Campbell's marathon walk. Her courage and stamina was unbelievable, and in comparison, my effort would seem like a stroll in the park. But the appalling sight of her feet - the soles blistered raw through wearing trainers - swayed my decision against using them. I would only change my boots for trainers at night just to potter around in, but that was all. The boots were half a size larger than my normal shoe, and thankfully, my feet had shown no signs of blistering.

* * * * *

The village of Kidasi was a small huddle of pre-fabricated houses. A blue hand-painted tractor stood in its owners front garden, and elsewhere, colourful flowering pots hung unwatered in the sun. I approached two of the houses but no-one answered my knock... not even the proverbial barking dog. Their small coffee-shop was padlocked, and outside a standpipe dripped water into a trough. I drank, then filled my sun hat and emptied it over my head - such was the heat of the day.

I trundled across a small road bridge spanning the dry

crusty bed of the Xerargaka river, having to step aside for a coach on its way north-east to the Troodos mountains. I doffed my hat to the cheering tourists, but with the driver offering no signs of a halt any thoughts of a quick collection were blown.

My stomach churned as I watched it spiral slowly up the mountain ahead towards Kedares. I rested before - and several times during - this murderous climb, praising the Lord when I reached its summit. The road then ferried me down through the greenery, and on my left, two kilometres from the village, there appeared an unusual church.

Agios Antonios was a seventeenth century building which featured a remarkably steep-pitched roof. Its icons had apparently been moved and were now preserved in Kedares' more modern church. But like the monastery, its doors barred my entrance and I had to be content admiring its structure from the outer limits. Just as the breezes had swirled in the mountains behind, here at the church, it was though they held their breath at the beauty of the flowers and trees in its cemetery.

As I walked into the village, two brothers sat watching my bedraggled form and bid me join them for a drink. Six more old-timers soon gathered around, making the friendly gestures of a drink and a kind word. They sat amused by my pigeon-Greek. Nevertheless, this was a new experience in their daily repetition of coffee-shop banter. I was news... a man with a mission, and I felt comfortable knowing they enjoyed my presence.

I sat with Patroclos and his brother on a bench, again listening to a lament for the exodus of village youngsters to the major towns. A story that echoes the sadness in most outlying villages. Theirs is a life of bitter-sweet memories; of days when families were bonded by generations of traditional values. But working the land no longer appeals to the young... the ties are broken now, and the old people - still proud and unyielding - know their demise will cast a terminal shadow over true Cypriot life.

'Right there!' Patroclos waved his cane up and down the street. 'Christos and I would play violins. Everyone sing, dance... Such happy times.'

One of the men reminded him of Nicosia, and he seized upon the chance to tell me all about them playing violins in a concert there. A second fizzy orange arrived for me, my money politely refused by the lady that brought it on a customary tray. I sat there baking in a tee-shirt, while the men around me looked cool and relaxed in thick sweaters and jackets, their faces and hands the colour of burnished gold.

With handshakes all round, I eventually said my goodbyes and battled on up the hill from the village. It was mid-day when I rested again some fifty metres short of a taverna advertising food. I had removed my pack, massaging the stiffness from my shoulders when a car appeared. Dorathy and her friend Richard had been out all morning searching for me. We decided to eat in the taverna, and for the first time in two days I enjoyed the luxury of a cooked meal.

The previous night as I camped in the Diarizos valley, she and Dimitrios - a doctor from the hospital - had searched the roads above the river without success. This morning she'd insisted on finding me to ensure all was well. Over lunch we thought a change of plan was necessary: a determination would be made by the charity to find me accommodation whenever possible in my last village of the day. We agreed this should be discussed in more detail upon my arrival in Galataria, where I was due to meet Doctor Phylactis again at his parents' house.

I continued to climb, taking a right fork in the road towards the region's most eastern community, Agios Nikolaos. Despite its name this was another Turkish-Cypriot village, and although inhabited, no-one ventured into its streets to witness my arrival; even dogs lay in silent distress, tethered in the hot sun. I felt an unusual apathy for the place. Wrong, I know, because north of the village stood a thirteenth century church, Archangelos Michael, which held a decorated marble slab and font. But I had little, or no luck with churches; the majority were locked when visiting them during the day. And besides, walking due north at this point was well outside my route.

Mount Olympus soared into a cloudless sky, its radar station shining like a giant white golf ball in the distance. I retraced my steps, strangely aware that although I now stood seven hundred metres above the Mediterranean sea, the rock formations around me had once exploded from the ocean's floor. In the Mesozoic era, Cyprus consisted of two small islands which fused together during an enormous underwater eruption. The volcanic masses solidified, thus forming these foothills around the Troodos mountains. It seemed ironic that nature had once joined this beautiful island... only for man to divide it again with bloodshed.

Nine thousand years of history are scattered over this island, and in the rocky veins beneath its skin still lie the weapons and bones of forgotten armies. Yet walking alone in its mountains and valleys, one only embraces peace and tranquillity. Nature created this island... and only she would ever destroy it.

A few kilometres south-west I found Pretori surrounded by olive groves and almond trees. The tiny hamlet lay in slumber, its afternoon siesta deepened by the lullaby of whistling birds. In the main street two donkeys stood tethered to a pole, their tails swishing a welcome as I approached. They were well cared for by the *papas*, upon whose doorstep I unceremoniously slumped.

My right shin was extremely painful by then, and sitting there rubbing in embrocation the door suddenly opened at my back and I almost toppled inside.

'Hero poli?' laughed the priest. He was a small man - most suited to the diminutive church I had passed earlier. A dark bushy beard matched his sombre robes, which were in stark contrast to the kindness of his smile and friendly blue eyes. He looked on in concern, asking if I needed help - then just as quickly returned inside the house for a Coca-Cola. The priest sat beside me on his doorstep, smiling as I thanked him by draining the bottle.

He insisted I stay for a while, and I sat watching with interest his slow methodical movements as he fed and watered his donkeys. Before I left, I tried to ask if he had knowledge of the remains of any Roman villas in the area.

'Ne! Ne!' he cried, excitedly. 'You must go to the sea at

Kato Paphos and Kourion.'

I understood, and thanked him for his hospitality, disappointed that my own mixture of Greek words and gesticulations had failed miserably, for Pretori village is said to be named after Prator, a Roman general who supposedly built a villa here. But given my linguistic skills I doubt if it would ever be found. I walked on, puzzled by the thought of why a Roman might reside so far from their strongholds near the sea.

The Romans had twelve cities on the island: Paphos (its capital), Arsinoe (formerly Marion), Kourion, Amathus, Kition, Salamis, Carpasia, Kyrenia, Lapithos, Soloi, Chytroi (Kythrea) and Tamassos. All but two were large coastal areas: Chytroi, built near the island's most prominent spring - and Tamassos, an important mining area. Both, however, were a considerable distance north-east of this small village, and apart from evidence of a Hellenistic temple that seemed to have continued into the Roman period, little else has been discovered above the lower reaches of the mountains. Prator's villa, therefore, remains a mystery.

The sun was now a fiery menace on this open road, yet the heights create their own cooling breezes and soon I had reached Filousa. This was a similar place to Pretori: a mixture of ruined, renovated and modern houses, where birds sang in abundance and swallows darted to and from deserted barns. I stopped only once to replenish my water supply at a stand-pipe, before walking through the empty streets in search of a track that would shorten my distance to Arminou.

Goat bells tinkled on the hillside as I drifted lazily down

into the valley, pausing to savour the smells and scenes that changed with every turn like a child's kaleidoscope. Butterflies danced around me and a pair of hawks floated aimlessly on the breeze. I found shade under a carob tree, eating an apple given me by the priest while I consulted my maps. I had been travelling almost seven hours - a considerable improvement on yesterday's trek - but from crossing the Diarizos river below to my overnight stay was another steep, twisting climb. I was not looking forward to it. My lack of sleep had taken its toll, and for the time being I was happy to rest and scan the rooftops of Arminou from this side of the valley.

My track saved a wide loop in the road, bringing me out just short of two bridges that ran parallel over the river. The old bridge had served the village for many decades, but its narrow capacity suited laden donkeys - not modern vehicles. An adjacent road-bridge now carried the traffic. From here, I was only four kilometres away from Arminou... the climb made it seem like four hundred. I would make it in a series of stop - starts, walking with numerous rests in between, whereby I adopted a hands on knees posture whilst gulping in the mountain air. The method worked for me and I used it daily, shortening or lengthening my paces according to the steepness of terrain or my general fatigue.

Griffon vultures are known to inhabit the island, and at times I felt like their prey sinking down at the roadside. Near the village I sat among the wild flowers casting a tentative glance upwards at the sound of flapping wings. It was a scavenger all right... but merely a low-flying magpie.

Arminou's mid-eighteenth century church of Stavros held

a silver-gilt plaque of Christ on the Cross, which locals maintain had one night mysteriously made its own way from Souskiou, a village in the southern reaches of the valley. It is said that harmony would never be the same between the two villages - but I found nothing but friendship at Arminou. As I crested the ridge, two pretty schoolgirls ran to greet me. Nadia had even remembered my name from the radio bulletins.

'Come, meester Petros,' she said, with all the wisdom of her mother. 'You must stay and rest with my grandma. She will look after you very well.' She and her friend Tereza, linked arms with me amid fits of giggling, and playfully frog-marched me to the coffee-shop. I was done for. My tee-shirt and trousers clung to my body and sweat dripped freely from my brow. The girls' indifference to the heat was amazing. Nadia wore a shirt, leggings and boots under a thick woollen anorak, while Tereza sported a track suit zipped up to her neck, and white trainers... both were perfectly cool and happy.

I collapsed into a chair, watching the last rays of sun burn away from the village while Nadia spoke excitedly to a lady standing in the coffee-shop doorway. A meal was duly arranged before the girls left, promising to return later when my room was ready at grandma Petrides' house. I surveyed my dining place and the charming people, therein.

The room was neat and tidy, its traditional furniture at one end with the exception of six chairs. These were occupied by three men: one each to sit on... and one apiece to lean on for snoozing. This they all did, snoring in perfect harmony around the room's centrepiece - and their favourite winter companion - a pot-bellied stove! It

Baking flaounes

sizzled... they snored... and everyone glowed red in the heat.

I opted for a table away in the far corner, and minutes later the old lady produced a fine Greek salad with lots of toasted *halloumi* cheese, two huge tomatoes, a sprinkling of olives and several chunks of freshly baked bread. I asked for a small beer and she gave me a large, nodding and smiling towards the stove as if to say, 'You'll need it!' I did indeed... drinking two before Nadia returned.

The charm of these men and the lady of the house lay, as ever, in their natural kindness and generosity. I was not allowed to pay for my meal, the men had apparently done so through Nadia hours before my arrival. Not wishing to disturb them I thanked the old woman, promising to return later once I had settled in at the Petrides' house.

Nadia and Tereza led me down a narrow lane that threaded between whitewashed cottages and rose scented gardens, informing me of their future ambitions. Tereza would be a runner. 'A famous athlete,' she said.

'And Nadia?' I asked. 'What about you?'

She stopped in her tracks, thought for a moment or two with hands on hips, before declaring: 'Well, first I will look after my grandma, and later, perhaps, children.' Then catching me completely off guard, she asked. 'What do you do... other than walk?'

'Oh! Like Tereza, I run sometimes... especially when my wife chases me.'

They were still giggling as we approached the house,

Nadia dashing ahead shouting her grandma. She paused in the lane long enough to kiss an old man unloading his truck, then raced on to embrace her grandma who stood waiting at the gate.

The man was in his seventies and handled the fifty kilo bags of cement like boxes of potato-crisps. I offered to help - but thankfully he refused, saying I should go on to the house. Grandma Petrides fussed over me, like grandma's do, and ushered me into a large section of the house which surrounded a pleasant courtyard, shaded by orange and lemon trees.

My room was being aired by two cradles of hot coals she had used earlier for baking. It contained two single beds and a double with brass bedsteads painted blue, a sturdy wardrobe with an orange suitcase on top and a beautifully carved dresser that almost touched the high wooden beams. This was adorned with pictures of the Virgin Mary and a small round tray holding a candle. The bed linen was fresh and spotless, and I gratefully accepted the firmness of the double bed.

Wherever her grandmother went Nadia followed, holding her hand, gazing at her endearingly and hanging on to her every word. As if reassuring me that I was nothing less than an honoured guest, she translated to me everything the old lady uttered.

Grandparents, particularly grandma's, are idolized by the younger children as they play an important role in their upbringing. Such open love and devotion is wonderful to see, but the habits of modern society are increasingly widening the gap between these generations. Sadly, one wonders how long it will last?

At the grandfather's invitation, I washed and shaved in their bathroom then joined him to eat *soutzouko* and raisins over another beer. His wife had prepared several trays of *flaounes* which Nadia said they would bake early next morning. It was this glorious aroma that awoke me. I had slept like a baby for ten hours, waking only once with my right shin reminding me of the day's journey.

By six o'clock I was dressed and my kit packed ready to go. I ventured outside just as Loizos was placing the last tray of *flaounes* into a huge oven. In the house, grandma was wrapping the freshly baked pieces into sheets of silver paper. I suddenly felt ravenous as I helped carry the finished trays in to her, and was rewarded for breakfast with lemon tea and a generous portion of bread, lightly spread with home-made jam.

Back in my room I discovered two hot loaves neatly wrapped in foil beside my backpack. And even before I could leave, the old lady pressed another gift into my hand: a brightly coloured tee-shirt. I was humbled by their refusal of money - something which I came to realize was a natural trait in Cypriot hospitality.

CHAPTER 3

NEAR DISASTER

The morning sky glittered, and fields came alive with colour as a breeze ruffled the heads of sleeping flowers. I saw no-one... but within this delicate fusion of beauty and light, I was never alone. There was magic in the silence: a serenity gifted to man - yet seldom cherished. And here, among the flowers and mountain pines, one could almost taste the freshness of the earth. This heady mixture, together with a smell of warm raisins from my backpack, tempted me to lie in nature's outstretched arms eating *flaounes*.

From the four alternative routes to my next village, I had originally chosen a pathway north-west of Arminou's cemetery. But it was a steep two hundred and fifty metre climb, and even at this early hour the sun determined a more sensible option. Although it meant a few extra kilometres, I decided to follow this main road to Agios Ioannis.

The village was situated on a winding slope, its Turkish-Cypriot community having fled northwards some twenty years before. As I approached through the olive groves, my hopes were raised at the sight of a freshly-painted cottage. It was locked and bolted, however, its bright green shutters closed to the sunlight. The garden stood forlorn: waist high in weeds and brambles, its only softness lay in a handful of poppies. I continued up the hill towards the main square.

Greeted by the noise of chattering sparrows I paused to rest, only to be startled by a lame dog which suddenly emerged from a derelict house. I called him. He stopped in his tracks, unable to determine the tone of my voice. It was a large dog with a handsome face; its big brown eyes, sad and glazed with hunger, looked at me almost in slow motion as if the simple effort of turning would be its last. Its legs and body were void of flesh - so emaciated, that the head seemed completely alien to its skeletal frame.

'Here boy!' I patted my leg. 'Let's see what I can find for you.'

He remained motionless. I released the straps of my backpack, and as if I was about to stone him, he began cowering away.

I unwrapped the *flaounes* and its sweet aroma reached him some five metres away. Then placing a small piece on the ground I retreated, calling to him quietly in Greek. This time he came... swallowing it whole. Having broken all the bread into small pieces I scattered them on the ground and left him to feast. I was sure grandma Petrides would not be offended... after all, his need was much greater than mine.

Agios Ioannis was a thriving village before the Turkish invasion, now it lay parched and desolate. An old eucalyptus tree towering over the square, looked down on streets that reflected images of music, wine and childrens' laughter. The sadness of war is such, that homes and memories are not forgotten... but left here to die in the sun. I took a long drink from my flask before retracing my steps.

The dog waited, slowly rising as I drew near. All the bread had disappeared, though he still eyed me cautiously as I searched for a container. I emptied the rest of my water supply into a dish and once more he came to my feet. This dog was the first animal I had seen in such a heartrending condition - it would not be the last. He lapped at the cold water, looking up at me only once as I walked away.

At this point I was barely three kilometres from the Paphos/Nicosia boundary, and in the north valley spanning the Xeros river was the Roudias bridge. Dated to medieval times, its restored double-decker construction spans over the creek, but again this was out of the confines of a route I strictly adhered to. I glanced at my watch, disappointed to see that it had taken me almost two hours to walk five kilometres. The pain in my right shin also outweighed an interest for the Middle Ages, so I left Agios Ioannis to rest in peace with my four-legged friend.

On the eastern side of this valley nestled a small neighbouring village. It was barely a kilometre away, but even as I followed a narrow track down the mountain I knew it would probably be a fruitless journey. It eventually led me to the edge of a vineyard, below which, stood the remains of Malounta. There was no need to intrude... nothing stirred except for a breeze whispering to the olive trees.

I sat for a while nursing an aching shin, trying not to contemplate the climb back to the road. Some five hundred metres below my feet the sun glinted on the Xeros river; it hardly seemed possible that already its depth and flow had dwindled to a rippling stream.

Only five months before my arrival the November rainfall had been more than two hundred times the average in some areas, bringing a hundred and twenty million cubic metres into the island's dams. The highest this century. Torrential rainstorms caused endless power failures, and widespread flooding had left a trail of destruction. Seasonal crops were ruined, and main roads - although of good quality - suffered through inferior drainage. It is not surprising, therefore, that when the storms do strike, most of the highways disappear under water. On the other hand, unlike the disastrous situation in the United Kingdom regarding water preservation, Cyprus does lead the way among European and Mediterranean countries for its efficient utilization of rainwater.

The November floods not only cured a two year drought, but they closely followed the arrival in Cyprus of the reputed miracle-working 'Axion Esti' icon of the Virgin Mary. It was reported that an estimated one hundred and fifty thousand people visited the icon, which had been displayed in various churches on the island... no doubt a few of them prayed for rain. A miracle or not, these thoughts made me decidedly thirsty as I raised myself from the ground.

It was a difficult climb back to the road, before I found a kind and casual descent taking me south to the road junction I required. From here I could see the rooftops of Mesana lying in the next valley. I checked my map and scanned the fields for a path that would save me a long detour. Through the hazy sunlight I saw it winding towards me like a child's discarded ribbon, only to disappear again into the endless rows of grapevines.

I started out through a field of low-growing maquis: a thicket whose thorns repeatedly clawed at my trousers. The earth was like sand, filling my boots so that both progress and patience began to flag in the heat. Several times I found myself tugged backwards as branches snagged my pack. After a hundred metres I was forced to stop. Wiping the sweat from my eyes, I found that both village and path had now disappeared. I was in a hollow, and beyond was a small vineyard. Having reached the top of this incline, my relief at the sight of Mesana was short-lived. My only way forward was into a gully twenty metres below.

Skirting the field in a southerly direction I eventually found its lowest point. There was no going back now - I was too exhausted. The sun had scorched its way high overhead as I removed my backpack and prepared to descend the rock face.

It appeared to be roughly four metres down to the path. At worst, if no footholds were available, I thought it possible to lower myself at arms length then drop the remainder. I approached the edge, lowering my pack by its straps until I heard it clatter and roll onto the path below. A sturdy grapevine grew near this spot; ideal, I decided, for holding on to and easing myself down. I tugged at it, satisfied the trunk would hold firm. Now to check for a foothold in the rocks... I took one step too many. The soft limestone rock and soil began to crumble under my feet and I fell.

Desperately turning to clutch at the moving earth, I grasped a tree root which held for a few seconds... then I was gone - plunging out into space before the solid ground below hit me with sickening force. I lay in a heap, dazed and bleeding from elbows skinned by the rocks.

My only good fortune was to land on my feet, but in doing so, a searing pain tore into the side of my left knee. I sat for a long time in the dust cursing my luck. Every bone in my body seemed jarred to breaking point, and my first attempt at rising was futile. Eventually, with my back and hands pressed against the rock face I managed to lever myself upright. Then, swaying towards my pack like a drunk smitten with fresh air, I retrieved a crepe bandage and strapped up my knee. I rested several minutes longer before stumbling on towards Mesana... every step an agony.

Somehow, despite an aching body and painful legs I managed to smile at my dilemma. With no food or water, a knee swollen to twice its knobbly size and still six hundred and forty kilometres to go, I could barely put one foot in front of the other without falling over. Mesana was no more than two kilometres away... it was to take almost two and a half hours to reach.

In the coolness of stone-built houses most of its people lay in their afternoon siesta, unaware that at long last I was shuffling through the village's sun baked streets. At the *cafenion* I dropped my pack on the floor and slumped down at the nearest table. Apostolos, the coffee-shop owner, and two old-timers loudly disputing a game of *tavli*, immediately came to my aid. They treated me with great kindness.

One of the old men delved into my toiletry bag and produced a tube of ointment, but Apostolos waved him away brandishing a bottle of clear liquid. 'This very good,' he beamed, unscrewing the top. *'Zivania* make you run - no walk! Hold out, thank you,' he laughed, tapping me with the bottle.

I cupped my hands, and he filled them several times so I could rub the liquid into both legs before re-strapping my knee. It felt warm and soothing.

'Now we drink it!' cried Apostolos, half filling four glasses which we all clinked together in a friendly toast... *'yia mas!'*

I sipped, eyes bulging as the liquid fired my throat. Through my tears, his wife smiled a silent welcome as she presented a tray of mixed nuts, orange segments and sliced apple. We ate and drank - the game of *tavli* forgotten... I lost all track of time.

At the foot of the Diarizos valley, south-east of the village, lies the monastery of Agios Georgios. It's a fifteenth century building which reputedly holds several unrestored icons. I thought it wise not to check as the rotating coffee-shop made it difficult to even find the door!

To an unsuspecting traveller or tourist the effect of *zivania* on a relatively empty stomach is mind-blowing! It's a raw spirit manufactured by distilling fermented grapes. Wine growers are allowed to produce it - people may buy it to drink - but apparently, a law invented by the British prevents its transportation. Yet *zivania* appears in every village and town on the island.

I was to learn that it can be dangerous to drink because both pips and stalks from the grapes are crushed and distilled, thereby producing a quantity of wood alcohol. The villagers use it externally as a remedy for certain ailments, and drink it neat to prevent colds and flu... or so they say! It can certainly be likened to a lethal wine reported by a priest from Westphalia. He visited Cyprus in the fourteenth century and mentioned that, '... if a man were to drink a whole cask he would not be drunken, it would simply destroy his bowels...' A rather sobering thought as I bid my hosts farewell and floated up the hill towards Salamiou.

As a well-made road carried me to the village, heat shimmered from the asphalt and merged with columns of smoke from back-yard ovens. Everywhere, the ashes from burning wood still smouldered with the wonderful smell of Easter baking. I was now entering my fifteenth village: less than half of which had been occupied, the remainder being Turkish settlements now lying deserted.

It was here at Salamiou, where a strange and highly provincial stele of Herakles had been discovered. A mid-fifth century piece that seems to be based on the Greek athletic relief's of that period. The dedicator is named Aribaos - a Macedonian name - who appears to have been devoted to the cult of Herakles-Horus.

When I reached the square it was already mid-afternoon, and finding an empty chair in the shade I released my backpack and sat mopping my brow. At this point my pockets were light, having collected only a small amount of money for the hospital. I was more hopeful of Salamiou.

The local coffee-shop was always my first point of call for two reasons: firstly, some form of cool refreshment would be available, and invariably, someone knew the whereabouts of their *mukhtar.* He or she was my main target, as in their possession should be a letter of introduction. Every *mukhtar* in the Paphos region had now received an official notification from the District Officer, informing them of my date of arrival in their village. And this, together with the media publicity, was to make a remarkable difference to the amount of donations received.

Two retired gentlemen with nut-brown skin emerged from the coffee-shop and welcomed me to their village. As before, in spite of the heat of the day, both men wore suits. One with a shirt, vest and pullover - the other, while dressed in the same undergarments, sported a waistcoat any country squire would have been proud of.

I was pleased to be recognized. They had apparently seen my television interviews and heard our appeal on local radio, which was always a favourable sign. They also spoke good English.

'Stay, please! I go find *mukhtar.* You wait, please. I bring him here very quick,' said the younger man. I thanked him, and prepared to check my injuries.

The *zivania* had burned its way into my senses well enough but the pain to my legs was rife again. My left knee, swollen and inflamed, gave me cause for concern. Meanwhile, a curious smell rose from my boots where the *zivania* had seeped down... probably rotting my socks! I was too disturbed to even untie my laces, as by this time shin splints had produced two ugly swellings either side of my right shin. I took the small bottle of *zivania* that Apostolos had given me as my 'one for the road' and soaked two bandages before applying them to each leg.

The 'waistcoat' man watched me in silence, his dark eyes following the liquid as it went to waste. He smiled, shaking his head as if in disbelief and returned to the *cafenion*. A few moments later he appeared with a large glass of freshly squeezed oranges and cubes of ice. I was then touched by his observations of me. He offered his hand, warmly crushing mine, saying that I had courage to continue. 'All Cypriots must salute you,' he said, earnestly. 'May our new-born children always be grateful.'

In the days ahead, and more importantly over the next few hours, I came to appreciate his confidence. I remembered too, distant words of encouragement from an old schoolteacher: 'Whoever you are and whatever you're trying to accomplish, no-one should really accept the taste of defeat,' he would say... 'It's very bitter!'

I was here with a promise to help the unborn children of Paphos, and even if being my stubborn and dogged old self wasn't enough, I knew I could rely on the support and friendship of the village people to lift my spirits. They alone would pull me through.

The houses of Salamiou were scattered along the main road, portraying as most of these distant villages do, a wistful picture of forgotten times. The only outward sign of modernization is to glimpse a new terracotta roof and the brilliant whiteness of an ex-patriot's cottage. I could see nothing of this here, the most up-dated building appeared to be the church across the street. My companion informed me that it was almost a century old, and the village itself dated back three thousand years. Looking around I had no reason to doubt him.

'We have another church one kilometre east of here,' he said. 'Panagia Eleousa is from the sixteenth century. Would you like to see?'

'Er... No. I'd rather not,' I smiled. 'This one will do fine. It's much nearer.'

His bright eyes seemed troubled as if he might be offended. But I re-assured him, saying that I'd be honoured if he would show me his village, instead.

The Greek Orthodox church of Agia Varvara was an imposing sight. I picked up my camera hoping to have a few minutes inside, but its doors were locked - even to the five pretty girls who arrived bearing flowers for the Easter service. Seeing my camera they posed on the church steps, holding bunches of roses, carnations and garlands of wild flowers. They wore necklaces made of twine and threaded with bright yellow margarita... a perfect contrast to their jet-black hair. As they giggled at my attempts to speak with them in Greek, I saw Yiannis returning. His news of the *mukhtar* was not good.

It had been impossible to determine my time of arrival in each village, so this was a disappointment I faced on several occasions. In the event of the *mukhtar* not being available I would leave word at the coffee-shop, or sometimes with the priest so that these particular villages might forward their donations directly to the hospital. I had been in Salamiou more than an hour... it was time to venture on.

I filled my flask with ice cold water and gratefully accepted the two oranges Christos, the 'waistcoat' man, stuffed into my pack. He walked me down to a tiny shop which boasted a Co-op sign in its window, and pointing to the road beyond, wished me luck with another bone-crushing handshake. Just two kilometres further, the pain became so intense I was compelled to stop again.

From where I sat on the rocky summit, I surveyed the daunting route before me and seriously wondered about my sanity! Seven hundred metres below lay the vast expanse of the Xeros valley, and perched somewhere high on the next mountain was my last village of the day. Galataria appeared to be a near verticle climb from the river. I could have stayed there forever admiring the view, but realized this would never reduce its distance. A helicopter would have been welcome... two pain-killers had to suffice. I scrambled to my feet again and prepared to descend into the valley.

Thirty minutes later my path narrowed into a fork, and whilst I was heading north-west it seemed obvious to bear right. It was a choice that almost cost me dearly. After a few hundred metres the track veered sharply right and upwards again. I stopped, annoyed with myself for wasting precious time. Now, short of returning a fair distance back up the mountainside, the only way to reserve my energy was to negotiate a steep rocky incline to the valley floor.

I edged my way through boulders and razor sharp rocks down a ridge that was barely a metre wide in places. It was no more than a landslide of earth and stone that had solidified over the years and formed a giant chute from the mountain. On my right was a sheer drop into a gully seventy metres below. I favoured the left side which had leisurely, but still dangerous, grass-covered slopes.

Because of its steepness I was forced to inch down sideways or slither along on my backside. A normal descent proved impossible as the weight in my backpack would have pitched me headlong into oblivion had I tripped. Yet stumble I did... my leading foot sliding away on loose stones. Suddenly I was down on my back, my right leg wedged against a rock. I lay there like an upturned turtle flirting with disaster, praying the boulder I had slithered into would not roll me into the ravine.

Looking up at the sky from this precarious angle was no place for man or turtle. So, slowly easing myself away from the boulder to relative safety, I sat there exhausted, taking in long gulps of air. It wasn't until I reached the bottom of this hazardous chute that the scary situation affected me. I was so mentally and physically drained that my resistance crumbled. I threw down my pack and followed it on to the ground, propping myself against the trunk of an old carob tree. Something squeaked and rustled among its branches. A tree rat, perhaps, annoyed at my alien presence? I was too weary for anything else to bother me. All I needed at that moment was the wings of a bird to glide across this awesome valley and settle on the rooftops of Galataria in time for tea. Tea... now that was a pleasant thought. A cup of tea... or better still, an ice-cold beer. My mouth was dry... I was tired of walking... falling... I could do nothing but sleep.

Not even a breeze or distant bird song stirred the valley when I awoke. There was nothing but silence. Alone in a formidable wilderness makes a human being as vulnerable as any of God's creatures, and I'm sure Enlart, the

Agios Nikolaos church - Galataria

French traveller, thought likewise. Upon his visit to the island a hundred years before, he had described the Paphos region as the most desolate and inhospitable part of Cyprus. Of course, the island was so different during his journey. These valleys and mountains were lush and green in forestry, with a variety of animals roaming the dense woodlands.

I peeled an orange, and had the man himself been there to share it I'm sure his opinion would not have changed. As for me, I would never deny this breathtaking scenery. For each time I touched its wild beauty it was though I was gazing into the eyes of Aphrodite herself.

My snooze calmed splintered nerves, and although my legs still troubled me I was thankful to be back on easier terrain for a while. Sliding the chute had saved considerable distance but not time, and I knew my charity team, Doctor Phylactis and the people of his village, could well be awaiting my arrival now in Galataria.

I was confident of crossing the Xeros river, two kilometres ahead, but that was all. The remaining six or seven up to the village was another matter. Galataria's location was almost seven hundred and fifty metres above the valley, and hobbling onwards to its towering mass I had to determine a route through pathways that spread like white veins to its summit.

As I approached the river, subtle changes of colour tempered the harsh reality of the valley. Areas on the near side banks were cultivated with vineyards, and trees stood in wavering lines still laden with fruit. Soon I could hear the chug-chugging of a pump and the hiss from irrigation systems watering the fields. My track veered away to the north, which meant another detour before it looped back again to reach a crossing point of the river. Here I rested, cupping my hands into its cool waters and soaking myself to the skin. After re-strapping the bandages and adjusting my pack I waded across, looking only at the water filling my boots... anything to keep eyes and mind from the enormous climb ahead.

On the other side I clambered up the riverbank to find my pathway blocked by an extraordinary field of boulders. My dismay was short lived, however, for in the sandy earth near the water's edge I noticed the paw marks of a dog. If my instinct held true it would be a pointer: a dog used by most Cypriots for hunting. I followed the trail - and sure enough it led me along a small inlet to a path, which in turn, weaved its way up to the road I so desperately needed.

The day's journey was far from over but at least I was on the home stretch, and although my legs were hardly able to support me at times, the distance to Galataria slowly ebbed away. I whistled and sang, shouted encouragement - even abuse at myself... whatever it took to keep one foot moving in front of the other.

How often I was forced to stop I will never know. Sometimes I managed to climb forty metres, more often I struggled to make twenty. On an open road the heat is intense, and this one, without shade or shelter, seemed to spin me in circles as it spiralled upwards like a coiled spring. My only consolation was an occasional glimpse of the day's trek diminishing behind me. But as beautiful as it was, the sight of a jeep careering down towards me lifted my spirits even more.

Doctor Phylactis and his brother, Andreas, warmly shook my hand, asking me to climb aboard. 'Come,' the doctor ordered. 'We will take you up to the village. Everyone is waiting to welcome you.' He and Andreas stepped forward helping me to remove my backpack, surprised when I refused their offer of a lift.

'I need to make it on my own,' I told them. 'It's something I have to do on foot. Otherwise, there's no reason to continue.' I sensed their concern. 'Don't worry. After this I will rest all day tomorrow.'

'Endaxi... OK. If you're sure? But we must take your pack. It will help you a little.' Andreas heaved it into the jeep. 'Now, when you reach a small church on the right,' continued Phylactis, 'the village is just a short distance ahead.'

I thanked them, taking a long drink from my flask before waving them off.

An hour had passed before I reached the tiny church of Agios Nikolaos. The single-aisled building was constructed against a rocky outcrop, and originated from the mid-sixteenth century. Its interior, I was told later, measures just nine metres by four. I felt too shattered to investigate its murals as they had been ruined by smoke. My only interest lay in reaching Galataria, and that was a further three kilometres up the mountain slopes.

The doctor's remark about the village being near the church was, I'm sure, to keep me going. I should have remembered that the estimation of distance and timescale to a Cypriot is based from behind the wheel of a car. No-one walks anywhere in Cyprus... it's too much of a dangerous pastime!

I rounded yet another bend in the road and saw a cloud of dust flying as a randy cockerel chased hens around a straw-covered yard. It was a joyous sight. I rested for a few minutes to gather my strength, ruffled my sweat-soaked hair and prepared for one last effort to reach the village square.

From breakfast with Grandma Petrides in Arminou, to the outskirts of Galataria, had taken me more than eleven hours.

CHAPTER 4

EASTER IN GALATARIA

A crowd of people rose from their seats outside the *cafenion* cheering my entrance to the village. Dorathy, Betty and her husband Jim, Doctor Phylactis... along with his brother, cousins, brother-in-laws and half the village, it seemed - all waited to shake my hand. For me, reaching Galataria was crucial. At least I could rest my injuries now and hopefully resume in the morning. Doctor's orders soon ruled me out, however, when Phylactis insisted I stay with his parents that night and visit hospital the following day.

With the brief celebrations over, our party went to a simple village house where I met Thaleia and Agathoklis, the doctor's parents. The men brought tables and chairs outside, and we sat in a large courtyard discussing the remainder of the walk's schedule.

I was reluctant to change the original route, but my legs could hardly support my own body weight, let alone a heavy backpack for another seventeen days. It was decided, therefore, to reduce my burden to basic requirements. For the remainder of my journey the charity would attempt to secure overnight accommodation for me. We would either meet in my last village of the day, or a message would be left with the *mukhtar* regarding sleeping arrangements. With the exception of a sleeping bag, this relieved me of all my camping equipment. Even my spare clothes were catered for, with the charity collecting and laundering my gear whenever possible on a daily basis. This considerably lightened my load... all I needed now was some new legs!

Phylactis puffed on a cigar, poring over my maps with his father who knew the region well. They listed a few Turkish villages which were either a pile of stones, or lay in distant valleys swallowed by the waters of a dam. This meant only minor restructuring - nothing serious. The doctor listened intently to his father, translating his thoughts and observations to me in English which I scribbled down. It was not difficult to see their admiration for each other.

Born in Galataria, Phylactis had to leave his parents at the tender age of twelve in order to attend Secondary School in Paphos. He rented a room in the town, and upon completing this part of his education, served one year's national service in the army. He left Cyprus in 1967 and for the next five years studied at Athens University to obtain his M.D. This was followed by eight successful years in England, culminating with his appointment as Senior Registrar in two West Midland hospitals.

In 1980 he returned to the island to take up the position of General Surgeon at Paphos Hospital, and over the past fifteen years has, in post-graduate terms, covered a wide field of surgical training and accomplishments in London, Greece, America and Cyprus. Seeing him now in his own back yard dressed in jeans and sweater, he was just another son taking his father's advice.

Phylactis was a heavily built man, tall and handsome, with dark curly hair and a neat beard. He smiled easily. His eyes were blue and tranquil, yet his presence unwittingly demanded respect. There was an unmistakable aura about him. Later, even in the remotest of villages, the very mention of his name evoked praise and admiration, particularly from the older people. But today was Good Friday, and I was delighted to be in the capable hands of his parents for the celebration of Easter.

Agathoklis beckoned me to follow him, for neither he or his wife spoke a word of English. This should be fun, I thought. He opened the door to my room and courteously invited me in to look around.

It contained two single beds, each with fresh sheets and blankets. The thick stone walls were whitewashed and bare, with a light bulb hanging from the rafters without a shade. I left my pack on a solitary chair, thanking the old man as he locked the blue-painted doors behind us and we returned to the house. Phylactis had explained earlier that his parents would be going to church, and that his mother would cook me something later on for supper. Thaleia was already busy at the stove when we returned.

She had set a place for me at the table, upon which was a plate of *flaounes*. Agathoklis produced a bottle of Commandaria wine from the cupboard and, after pouring me a generous helping, proceeded to get ready for church. It was strange, but my communicative system worked very well with them. Language was no barrier... there was an instant rapport between us as though we had known each other for years. Thaleia would often laugh at my antics, yet even so, we related admirably.

The sky was already flooded with stars, bathing the streets in a radiance of light that cast pale shadows over the village. I watched from the gate as the old couple walked arm in arm, Thaleia turning to wave as they joined other villagers on their way to church. I wondered if my legs could muster another hundred metres? It was a rare opportunity to see a Greek Orthodox service at Easter time, perhaps my last. I headed for the washroom.

The shower was across the courtyard adjacent to an outside toilet, where soap, shampoo and clean towels had been left for me. Like most infrequencies, the warm cascading water was pure luxury. The general aches and pains from my first three days just trickled down a plug hole in the concrete floor. A vigorous rub down with a towel in the cool night air of Galataria works wonders for an ageing torso... my injuries apart, I felt remarkably healthy!

A sickle moon was lost in the star studded heavens, and a murmur of voices seemed to drift up from the valley as I entered the main street. I walked towards the church, but again the echoes followed me. Then I saw them... a trail of golden light stealing through the shadows. Villagers young and old walked slowly behind a priest, some holding candles that barely flickered in the still night air.

The priest, resplendent in his robes and snow white beard, chanted in a proud baritone voice. Directly behind him came four men with heads bowed. Each held a corner of a crimson sheet that represented the robe in which Christ was taken from the cross; it was adorned with a profusion of flowers from the gardens and mountain slopes. Small children waved as they passed by, and many villagers invited me to join the procession. I was

no longer a stranger.

At the church steps, the sheet was being held aloft so the congregation might pass beneath its canopy of flowers. I stepped aside into shadows steeped with the scent of lavender. These flowers, also known as myrophores, are associated with the name of the women bearing perfumes to Christ's tomb. They filled the air with a fragrance that ravished the senses.

I was content to watch and listen to the service from near the doorway, but as the congregation entered the church someone tugged at my arm.

'Ela! Ela!' Agathoklis was ushering me inside. He led me to a pew facing the congregation where a hundred pairs of eyes greeted mine. My clothes were inappropriate - but not frowned upon, except for a quizzical glance from the priest as he disappeared into the apse. Agathoklis quickly returned to his seat and the service began.

I remembered the village was said to be named after Galatarka, a lady whose goats produced a surfeit amount of milk; an image that also seemed to reflect through its church, Panagia Galatarousa... bearer of milk. Built in 1768, it contained several icons dated from the fifteenth century, but sitting there in the half-light I could not determine which of them graced the *iconostasi.* There were more than thirty. Nearby, a huge glass chandelier reflected crystals of light upon them, suggesting an expression of life to their solemn faces.

The bier was decorated in a mass of colour: lilies of the valley, carnations, deep-red roses, orchids and lavender that tumbled in abundance into the pastel shades of wild flowers. Almost every adult held a single bloom, while the children stood in a semicircle around the bier holding posies. Melodious voices rang out as two men chanted in turn: the richness of the younger man's voice complementing the wavering tones of the old. Their tempo was sweet and unhurried, soon to be accompanied by a third voice from behind the *iconostasi*. A curtain opened and the priest appeared. He walked sedately to the bier singing to the congregation, who responded in unity to his words. Although I was unable to interpret their poetic phrases, this simple ceremony left me enchanted.

Through the trees the stone walls of Panagia Galatarousa held a luminous glow under the stars. Weary, yet contented, I walked the old couple back to their house.

Thaleia prepared supper with measured efficiency. She was a small lady, her eyes the softened blue of cornflowers. Her dark green dress was protected by a long apron, below which, she wore customary leather boots. Her hair was partially covered by a black head-scarf, and around her neck draped a beautiful gold cross and chain. To me, she was kindness itself.

While her husband retrieved the bottle of Commandaria, Thaleia had large portions of *halloumi* cheese sizzling in the pan. This was for my salad, as they, like all the old folk in these distant villages, still maintained the traditional fast: seven weeks when meat, fish, eggs, cheese and milk, or any animal substitute is renounced in their diet. She and Agathoklis shared a simmering pan of beans and lentils, with a plate of tomatoes, cucumber and a bowl of black olives.

Halloumi is the national cheese of Cyprus. Made from

milk curdled with rennet, the whey is drawn off afterwards and the curd boiled in it. Salted and then seasoned with mint, it has a rubbery texture which is said to need an acquired taste in comparison to English cheeses. Mine was cooked to perfection.

The family Constantinides converged on us after supper for an amusing evening of verbal and gesticulate conversation in Greek and English. It was around midnight before I returned to my room. In Cyprus the dogs bark, roosters crow and donkeys bray at the most unnatural times. I slept for nine hours... immune to them all.

'*Kalimera*, Petros.' Agathoklis greeted me as I crossed the courtyard next morning. He stood combing his hair, but noticing my towel and toiletry bag, stood aside to let me wash at an outside sink. The water was cold... silky soft. I had stripped to the waist, and with typical Cypriot intrigue Agathoklis enquired about the long scar that curved under my shoulder-blade. Equally, he couldn't resist a question on the contents of my toiletry bag, taking particular interest in the shaving foam and disposable razors. He was a remarkable man: small in stature but strong and resilient in mind and body, despite being asthmatic.

At breakfast he took his daily medication in annoyance. His asthma probably caused by a lifetime of back-breaking work spent in the dusty vineyards. Like most bronchial disorders there were no outward signs of distress, but later, as he took me to the heights of Galataria, his breathing became harsh and laboured. Nevertheless, he persevered, and with the aid of his stick got there just ahead of me.

Agathoklis was an amiable character, still handsome and alert for his eighty years. I enjoyed his company... even the wry smile as I struggled behind him. A cooling breeze mellowed the sun, and at the coffee-shop Christakis - yet another relative - called us to join a friendly group of villagers. They handed me a generous donation for the charity. Back at the house, meanwhile, Thaleia was already preparing lunch.

Apart from our stroll into the village, I sat resting most of the day, which helped reduce the swelling and pain in my legs. So, rather than anyone come up to Galataria, take me to see the doctor and then drive back again, I contacted the charity. I would press on for two days until my route returned to the sea near the hospital. It was a risk that disappointed the old couple. I'm sure they thought I was staying for a whole week! Agathoklis had retired into the house, dozing at the kitchen table while Thaleia and I sat in the courtyard. I watched her with interest. She sat on a low, straight-backed chair, with a small bucket of water on her lap and a bowl on the floor beside her. The knife in her hand moved swiftly, slicing away potato skin quicker and finer than any modern peeler. Looking at Thaleia, I saw my own mother's hands and lightness of touch. She would work silently, always with her special bone-handled knife, dropping each perfectly peeled potato into an enamel bowl. Thaleia had that same dexterity: a brisk, yet seemingly unhurried way of making even the hardest task look simple. She cooked egg and chips for me but mainly, lunch was a huge dish of Greek salad with warm crusty bread and wine, followed by apple segments and oranges. I returned to my room later, with every intention of checking my maps but fell asleep. I was unconscious for three hours.

Andreas, Thaleia's schoolteacher son, called in at five o'clock suggesting we might have a quiet beer in the coffee-shop. It was full of familiar faces, all wishing to re-fill my glass at regular intervals. I remembered very little... suffering for it the next day as the sun was murderous.

Andreas had spent fifteen years in Rhodes studying and working as a teacher. When he and Phylactis were young men, his father had worked the land sixteen hours a day to help raise money for their education. Agathoklis could well be proud, not only of his sons but also his own achievements in helping them. Phylactis was now at the pinnacle of his medical career, and Andreas a highly qualified teacher in physics, chemistry, biology and mathematics.

This parental dedication to a child's future and well-being is an undying quest that symbolizes their ultimate meaning in life. The greatest tragedy of all for a Cypriot is to outlive any of their children. In a short space of time I had grown very fond of the old couple; it was not easy saying good-bye. Shortly after sunrise, I was tidying my room when Agathoklis tapped at the door. He had already filled up my flask with fresh water, and Thaleia was waiting with some oranges for my journey. I thanked them for their hospitality, but knew they were not seeking gratitude. The sadness in their eyes asked only a silent promise of me... that one day I would return.

It was Easter Sunday, and my day would begin by heading due north towards a neighbouring village. From there, my route would veer north-west to the southern fringes of Paphos forest and Pano Panagia, before returning south to Pentalia. A round trek of thirty kilometres.

I was pleased with my new lightweight pack because in little more than an hour the heights lifted another two hundred metres. With the sun already awakening the most shaded flowers, I passed through the village of Kilinia. Their dogs barked at my breathless form then loped across, tails wagging, to be fussed. The pointers came from a yard full of turkeys, goats, cockerels and hens, but unlike the poor creature in Agios Ioannis, they were well fed and watered. I drank from my flask without conscience.

These mountains and foothills fall into limestone terraces, and during the summer's endless heat when the land seemingly dies, this chalky landscape is flushed with a dense green network of vineyards. But now, as everything wild blossomed in a myriad of colours around me, the vines were lifeless. They stood like stumps of charcoal, black and unyielding against the bleached earth and stones. The fields were clearly indicated on my map but not the road taking me on, ever upwardly, north-west to Statos.

The area had been chosen to re-site and combine two villages into one: old Statos in the north-east, through which passed the main road to Panagia, and Agios Fotios that lay south-west. It was as though the residents of new Statos had also experienced a late night... everyone seemed to be sleeping.

The village was a maze of streets, and after wandering aimlessly in search of life-form I suddenly became aware of someone following me. A small boy was dragging something on a piece of string. As he drew near he began making a hissing noise, whipping the string around and shouting: 'He's got you!'

I smiled at him as the dead snake fell at my feet. He stared back, disappointed that I hadn't jumped out of my skin. This would have been a normal reaction had I not seen the game before, but instead, I picked up the snake pretending to eat it. His eyes, almost as black as his curly hair, widened in disbelief.

'Are you biting my friend?' he asked.

'Yes... I'm hungry.' I was teasing him, and he knew it. A smile lit up his face, and without a word he took my hand leading me to a nearby house. The reptile dragged behind us.

Yiannis was ten years old, and as he met with a scolding from his grandmother I prepared for a hasty retreat. His mother, however, trying hard not to laugh, assured me it was only because her son kept bringing the snake into the house. Eleni spoke excellent English and had taught Yiannis herself. I was offered *flaounes* and fruit, but settled for some fresh orange juice before continuing my journey.

Yiannis, with his snake in tow, escorted me to the road I wanted for the monastery and stood waving me out of sight. His friend was a large whip snake, one of the longest snakes in Europe. This one was almost two metres in length; its body was black and shiny with a yellowish belly. Yet despite their fearsome size, it is completely harmless. In fact, their presence is extremely useful around villages, helping to keep down vermin and even poisonous snakes which they kill by strangulation. Normally, the whip snake has a rounded snout, but Yiannis' playmate was headless... guillotined, no doubt, by a terrified villager.

Along an open track the sun turned my night of liquid refreshment in Galataria to sweat and discomfort. I learned that beer, wine and sun is a cocktail that should be avoided at all costs. My concentration wavered, and even though the track turned into a comfortable descent, I found myself floundering like a man lost in the desert. I settled on a crown of daisies watching a pair of crested larks who, it seemed, also wanted to play games. Earlier, they had appeared on the track scurrying along no more than a metre ahead of me. If I stopped, so did they. If I zigzagged along, they copied. Now, as I sat removing the support from my shin, they paraded up and down with impatience. Then as if to say: 'We must have worn him out!' they flew away. Shortly afterwards, I reached the main road to Panagia, along which, were two important monasteries.

The first, Agia Moni, is one of the island's oldest Christian foundations. Built on a site where once stood a Temple of Hera in Hellenistic times, it was abandoned in 1571. Since my previous visit some years earlier it had been extensively renovated. Now the monastery seemed to have lost its identity; it belonged to no particular era, other than the present. The surrounding areas flourished in vineyards and fruit trees, and I walked a ridge from where the land sprawled westwards in gently receding foothills towards the sea. Directly ahead loomed Paphos forest.

This dense greenery blankets the mountains and floods the Cedar Valley beyond. A mirror image of what Cyprus resembled in antiquity, before trees were felled for ancient ships and the melting of copper ores. Now the woodland covers just one-fifth of the island.

The forests of Paphos contain a great variety of trees, some of the more practical species appear to be: alder - used in furniture, barrel staves and plywood. Aleppo pine - probably the most common tree, is a resinous wood used for fruit boxes and general construction purposes. Cedar is a tree that grows in the higher altitudes of Mount Tripylos and around Kykko Monastery. This species: cedar brevifolia, is said to have been used as pit props in ancient copper mines. It is unique to Cyprus and now a protected tree. The golden oak is a bushy tree, characterized by its dark green leaves which are a golden yellow on the other side. Mainly used for parquet flooring because of its hardness, the wood also makes good fuel in winter.

Following centuries of forestry extraction and fire damage, the British occupation in 1878 rectified the problem by introducing proper controls. It was gratifying to see such lush foliage and hear so much bird life among the trees. Yet somewhat adversely, deep in a western ravine, another Turkish village had died. The faceless windows of Lapithiou stared up at the sky. No-one answered their plight... no-one, it seemed, ever would.

This was a cool and peaceful spot, where a welcome sign informed me of the Papaloukas Picnic Site. I dumped my pack on a wooden bench and sat under the pine trees studying my route. A second monastery was close at hand, but I decided this could be visited later in the day when I returned along the same stretch of road. My main concern was finding a short-cut to Asprogia, and although there was nothing visible on the map, I found it by chance. A steep downward path that led me through Mamoundali, another Turkish village, and up to the main road due west of Panagia.

I was now in the neighbourhood of ancient iron mines, where the church of Agios Epifanios was said to preserve an early sixteenth century icon of the Pantokrator, the Almighty: often symbolized as a half-figure of Christ in the central dome of a church. Except for the sound of its distant bell, Asprogia itself was peaceful. Before Turkey's invasion, the village was one of several where hundreds of Greek and Turkish Cypriots lived together in harmony. But through its main street I passed but a handful of people whose faces looked as jaded as mine. I rested for a few minutes at the roadside before walking on to the village where Makarios was born.

In Pano Panagia I sat outside the Green Leaf restaurant, removed my boots and socks, and ordered *kleftico* with Greek salad and fresh orange juice. This was by far my largest village to date, its population once numbering three thousand. At present, according to the restaurant owner, this figure had dwindled by two thirds. I chose not to reason why but sat enjoying the wonderful meal he spread before me.

The village was edged by limestone cliffs, and shadowed by the imposing backdrop of Paphos forest. It was here in 1913 that Panagia beheld its favourite son. Born Michael Mouskos, one of four children, he was just another boy herding goats in the forest until he entered Kykko Monastery as a novice. By the age of thirty-seven he had adopted the name Makarios (Blessed), entered the political arena and was elected Archbishop of all Cyprus. Ten years later he became the first President of the Republic.

He was a charismatic figure: a political opponent of the British, an obstacle to the Turkish plans for the partition of the island - but worshipped like a god by the Greek

Cypriots. Makarios died in 1977, and his wish was to be buried at Throni, a place high in the mountains above Panagia. His guarded tomb stands at the spot where villagers used to pray for rain; amazingly enough, in the normal blistering heat of August there was a heavy downpour at the time of his funeral. Greek Cypriot eulogistics attributed this rain to the tears of God.

I had previously visited his tomb, the two museums in his honour and a large statue in the square, yet found his childhood house much more atmospheric. As always, my purpose was not to digress too much but to call on the village *mukhtar.* I was informed that he and most of the villagers were presently packed inside the church of Panagia, hosting a government official and other dignitaries from Nicosia. I decided not to wait, and ambled down a hill towards the second monastery.

CHAPTER 5

PERPATITOS

My attention was mainly focused ahead, or on what lay around me, so to pause and look back happened too infrequently. This was Mount Royia, one of the most westerly spurs of the Troodos mountains. It stood almost one thousand metres above sea level, and retracing my steps now unfolded spectacular panoramic views.

The monastery was busy with tourists, but I found an empty table and sat under a shaded terrace. At the cliff edge stood a huge pinus brutia tree, bearing a sign that indicated it was one hundred and ten years old. Beneath its branches - with hot coals and sparks threatening its very existence - a young man roasted chickens on a three-pronged spit. He divided his time with the chickens and serving nuts at a nearby stall; in between he also worked in the restaurant helping his in-laws over the busy Easter period. Curious at seeing me arrive with a backpack, he left his chickens and introduced himself as Socrates. His English was clear and precise.

'Why do you walk?' he asked, cheerfully. 'My cousin has cheap car-rental in Paphos. I telephone him for you...' He went to move away and I caught his arm.

'Wait! No thank you. I have to walk because it's for charity.'

'Charity? What is this... this charity?' But then, before I could answer. 'Ah! You have no money. No problem. I will fix something. I'm sure my cousin will...'

'Please,' I interrupted. 'Sit down and I will explain.'

Socrates looked genuinely puzzled until I told him about the hospital's needs and my reasons for walking. A look of wonder and admiration came over his swarthy features... then suddenly he remembered the last of his roasting chickens and fled. I was writing notes when he returned with a broad smile on his face.

'Now I know you!' he said, loud enough for everyone around to stop eating. 'I hear on the Radio Paphos. They call you, er... *Perpatitos* - the walker. Do you want some chicken? It's very good... Hey! I like your boots, man. How much do they cost?'

The words flowed in one breath, and a Scottish couple at the next table almost choked with laughter on their salad. I thanked him for his offer of food but suggested a drink of orange would do nicely. He brought it on a tray with some pistachio nuts, steadfastly refusing my money. Socrates kept eyeing my boots, nodding with satisfaction when I told him they cost thirty English pounds. I asked about the monastery, and he launched into a verbal assault of information that even left the Scots breathless.

Accordingly, Panagia Chrysorrogiatissa - Our Lady of the Golden Pomegranate - was founded in 1152 by a monk named Ignatious who, upon salvaging an icon of the Virgin Mary from a fire, heard a voice telling him to build a sanctuary for it at Mount Royia. The entire monastery and its church was restored and rebuilt in 1770 by Bishop Panaretos. It is to a plan which most monasteries reproduce without deviation. This includes a central courtyard enclosed by a two storey building, with dormitories generally situated on the upper floors, and souvenir shops, offices and workshops below.

I was writing furiously, trying to keep pace with Socrates while a smartly dressed Frenchman and his daughter listened, enthralled. The Scots had also forgotten their lunch, leaning towards us so as not to miss a word.

Socrates sensed his captive audience, smiling as he continued to explain the wonders of one of the icons made by a famous icon painter from Crete, John Cornaro. He paused only once when a prospective customer came to his stall. '*Parakalo*? Yes please?' he shouted, hands held out appealingly. The tourist walked away and Socrates shrugged his shoulders, soon stimulating our imagination again with another of the church's treasures: a holy shroud embroidered by Russian Orthodox priests in 1797.

I emptied my glass of orange juice, thirsting at the non-stop barrage of information. Before I could turn a page to write he had moved on to the subject of wine.

'On the eastern side of the monastery the monks have about fifty donums of vineyards which, to you my friend,' his hand clasped my shoulder... 'is almost sixty-seven thousand square metres.'

The Scotsman let out a low whistle. 'My... that's a few grapes to be sure, laddie,' he said.

Without hesitation, Socrates continued: 'Their Agios Andronicos wine is produced from the Xynisteri vine - white grapes. But my favourite, Agios Ilias, comes from a local black grape variety that grows on the slopes between two and five hundred metres higher than the monastery. The monks named it after the mightiest peak of the mountain.' Socrates gave a little cough. 'You may buy it at the monastery... but not now,' he quickly added. 'The fathers are busy gathering for a service.' Clasping his hands, he gave us his best smile. 'Please allow me... I think we have some for you to see in the restaurant!'

I thanked him for his illuminating story. Socrates gave a little bow... but then more urgent matters came to bear as both the French and Scottish parties showed their interest in purchasing some wine. It was time to take my leave.

At the southern end of the monastery I found a small clearing in the pines where dappled shadows fell upon a handful of stone crosses. Their inscriptions were brief, revealing only that here was a final resting place for the monks.

In a short time I was back at the picnic site, my painful legs again needing attention. I re-strapped my knee, and was massaging the last drops of *zivania* into my shin when a pair of hoopoes fluttered to the ground, nearby. They were elegant birds: pinkish-brown, with striking black and white bars across their body, wings and tail. The crest of one bird was raised in a large pink fan, the tips of which were speckled like splashes of black ink.

As their thin curving bills raked the pine needles for insects, a low 'pou-pou-pou' sound occasionally filled the air. This distinctive call, likened to their Greek-Cypriot name, poupouxos, means 'where? where? where?'

When they flew away into the green curtain of pines, it was in a slow, undulating motion that enhanced the sleek colours of their plumage. They cried again, 'pou-pou-pou', and sitting there biting into the sweetness of an apple, I was reminded of the hoopoe's connection to the swallow and the nightingale in Greek mythology. A gruesome tale - even by Classical standards - of Tereus, who fell in love with the voice of his sister-in-law, Philomila.

She resisted his advances so he raped her. When his wife Procne discovered this, Tereus promptly cut out her tongue to stop her talking. Procne then revenged his misdeeds with a savagery of her own: she murdered their child, Itys, serving him up to Tereus for supper. Filled with rage Tereus began to chase the sisters with an axe, but the gods intervened. They turned Philomila into a nightingale, whose song forever mourns the death of a child; Procne into the swallow that twitters but never speaks; and Tereus became a hoopoe, who cries in pursuit of them both, 'pou-pou-pou'... 'where? where? where?'.

The apple had suddenly soured. I heaved on my pack again and followed the main road towards Pentalia, my last village of the day.

From the monastery of Agia Moni the flowing lines of fruit trees appeared like legions of Roman soldiers pouring down the hillside. I circled them, skirting the eastern ridge above the Ezousas valley until the banks of wild

Donkey at Statos

flowers faded into a landscape scarred with iron slag-heaps. I was entering the old village of Statos.

On a hill to my left a few houses raked the skyline; most had stumbled into mounds of rubble between grassy hollows. A lone donkey grazed among the shrubbery, and over the blackness of the quarry hovered a pair of kestrels. Their tails were spread, wings moving rapidly as they searched for prey. The village was filled with the cooing of nesting pigeons, and near its end I found another donkey tied to a pine tree.

He had plenty of shade but no water, and grew instinctively afraid as I approached him. He was badly marked on the forelegs: strips of his brown coat skinned back to the flesh like a torn sleeve; the same white scar tissue that streaked his flanks. I unbuckled my flask, letting him see a trickle of water in the palm of my hand. With a curious tilt of his head he watched me a step closer. I was almost touching his whiskers, but the fear remained in his eyes and he backed up against the tree. I emptied half of my flask into his water-bucket and sliced him an apple before leaving. He would touch neither until I moved away.

The road to Pentalia follows a high ridge, and as one valley appears, so another falls between distant hills. While the day's heat simmered in the earth, this undulating terrain lay like a sleeping dragon; its breath forming a fiery haze that rippled the landscape. My stretch of road descended southwards on an easy plane back to the sea. But that was another day's trek, all I needed for now was a resting place. It was difficult enough to carry a pack and shuffle along on one leg... my problem was limping on both! I reached Pentalia at six o'clock.

At the side of the church Easter games were drawing to a close with a village tug-of-war. I enquired after Yiangos, and a kindly white-haired man stepped from the crowd inviting me to his office for a drink. We entered a small supermarket, closely followed by a dozen children wanting to buy his sweets. *'Eimaste kleisti!'* he cried, indicating the shop was closed as they jostled through. He winked at me before teasing them again by pointing to his watch. But he happily served them while I waited in his office.

It was a tiny space, with a narrow desk and one chair set among the shelves of bleach and toilet cleaners. Yiangos presented me with seventy pounds from his village fund then, aware of my considerable discomfort, insisted on carrying my pack across to his house. Most of the family gathered there, everyone having heard of *'Perpatitos'*, a scruffy sweat-soaked Englishman who had come to stay with them. The house was large, but even so, with this number of children and adults I could hardly envisage where I might be sleeping. Later that night it came as quite a surprise.

Sozos, whom I took to be the eldest son, led me through the kitchen to a small washroom where I freshened up before joining the family for an evening meal. Sozos and I talked at length about England, the family and his boutique shops in Nicosia, then drank a little beer watching the Easter services on television. Much to my embarrassment, the next thing I remember was Yiangos waking me up. He and his son were most amused. Everyone else it seemed had returned home and gone to bed.

A handful of stars were barely visible through the low clouds, and with no street lighting the blackness of night was almost complete. Yiangos led the way with a torch. He was closely followed by Sozos, carrying my pack, while I constantly tripped up at the rear. At first I thought we were on our way to a neighbour's house, but after crossing the road and climbing a few steps, Yiangos unlocked the door of an unusual building. It was not until he switched on the light that I realised my bed was in the main classroom of the village schoolhouse!

I was too tired to notice my surroundings. When the two men left I undressed by torch light, forgetting even to lock the door. A single bed had been freshly made up for me, its springs twanging to breaking point as I clambered aboard. I slowly sank until the bed resumed the form of a hammock. Somewhere in the night a lonely dog howled... I slept without dreaming.

The sun was already peeping through the windows when a chorus of sparrows awoke me. My sleepy eyes searched for a chirpy soul much louder than the rest... he was perched on the top of the blackboard. As I lay studying the contents of my 'bedroom' I was distracted by the bird flying up to its nest. This simple instinct created a touching and most extraordinary scene. A portrait of Jesus hung over the blackboard, and directly above, the sparrow had built its nest in a small alcove. From where I lay my angle of vision transformed the straw into a crown of thorns. Then, as sunlight played on the high windows, its radiance touched the face of Christ... and for one remarkable instant the anguish in His eyes fell upon me. A drifting cloud brushed over the sun, and just as quickly the moment passed. It is difficult to explain, but before I left that room no matter how many times I looked at the portrait... His gaze was never the same.

I levered myself out of the bed, which now retained its hammock-like shape, and noticed the classroom had been partitioned. Near the door stood a cabinet bursting with medical supplies. A few chairs and benches were strewn around, and as I moved, a mouse rapidly disappeared through a hole in the floorboards. Cautiously, I tested the weight on my legs. There was no pain or stiffness, so I ventured around the back of the school in my pyjamas to find a place to wash.

The morning was bright and cool with masses of cumulus cloud searching the sky. It seemed a perfect day for walking. On paper, my route appeared as a twisting causeway of red and yellow lines that meandered through pine woods, wild olive and almond trees. A much-needed respite from previous treks. In reality, however, the day held a much more sinister threat.

I observed from my notes that the village church might still contain an unusual icon of the Virgin and Child, portraying Elijah and the ravens on its reverse side. And along the road above Pentalia, ancient tombs could also be seen in the cliff-face. But as interesting as these fragments of history might be, they were, in my present condition, too time-consuming to pursue. It was seven-thirty, and I was already late leaving the village.

North of the school, a road dipped through rocky terraces to the far reaches of the Sterakovou stream. From the top of the gorge it seemed so near to my next village that should I have cast a stone it would surely clatter onto the rooftops below. But there's no such respite for the walker. In the mountains and foothills distance cannot be measured as a bird flies; you are fated to tread the pathways and tracks in never-ending spirals. This one was no exception. As the morning sun caressed the Xeros river, I walked a road that coiled itself around the gorge, down through olive groves and fig trees into the vineyards of Agia Marina.

There was a wall expertly rendered with chippings of white stone enclosing the cemetery, and flowering fields led me to the village beyond. White anthemis and the daisy-like yellow similoudi flirted in the breeze with rows of purple thistle and wild poppies. Only Mother Nature could portray such beauty... or was this the way of Aphrodite? For it is said that grass and flowers sprang from the earth wherever she trod, forever to adorn the Cypriot fields in springtime. It seemed that my every step followed in her footprints.

The residents of Agia Marina were fifty strong. I was invited to share a cooling drink in the shade of the *mukhtar's* house, where a few villagers gathered upon hearing of my arrival. The genuine interest and friendliness I experienced never ceased to surprise me, and most times I felt great disappointment in having to move on. This, apart from two exceptions, was one of those days.

As I crossed the road bridge a few kilometres into the bowels of the gorge, the sound of gunfire echoed through the trees. I stopped, watching the panic in a flight of finches. Their greens and yellows, and the scarlet faces of the goldfinch all desperately seeking refuge in the pines.

There came another report... much nearer this time, and from a crevice in the rock face a noisy family of crows flew down like black tattered rags, skimming the road ahead of me. It was then that I saw him. Where a fire had destroyed a large area of forestry, the sunlight glinted on the barrel of his gun through the gutted trees. He was high up on the ridge, and although out of range, was firing in my direction.

On a horseshoe bend near the main road another shot rang out. This time a hail of pellets clattered into the trees behind me. I shouted - more in annoyance than fright - and from the undergrowth emerged what appeared to be a young mercenary. He was dressed in a heavily camouflaged suit and hat, with belts of ammunition criss-crossing his chest like a Mexican bandit. I started to lecture him on his stupidity of using the gun near the road, but he just shrugged his shoulders pretending not to understand. He merely slotted another cartridge in the breech and moved away. His target was undoubtedly the finches, which infuriated me even more.

These, and other small birds, like *strouthos*, are shot mostly for sport. But I had seen them eaten in tavernas, their tiny bodies served as a delicacy and eaten with a sickening crunch as both meat and bone is devoured.

The clouds had faded away in the sun as I trundled into Amargeti. I sat under the tall pines outside the coffee-shop, its tables and chairs surprisingly filled with youths too pre-occupied in playing cards and *tavli* to notice a crotchety alien. Perhaps it was this ill-mood that saw me write in my notebook:

'The first British archaeological expedition to Palaepaphos visited this village and escavated a form of sanctuary, Opaon Melanthios, the patron god of shepherds. In 1888 their booty was shipped back to the English museums... could it be from the silent, unsmiling stares around me that I am to blame? Somehow, the sight of a hunter blasting small helpless birds has soured my feelings. I think it's time to drink up my lemonade and leave...'

Back on a southerly route the road was asphalt, and like me, had begun to melt in the mid-day sun. I was labouring, and although reluctant to take pain-killers unless absolutely necessary, I had no option. These, together with my restful nights, thankfully kept me mobile. Yet I made no more than a kilometre from Amargeti before resting at a bus shelter. I studied my maps - lest someone should think I was waiting for a bus - and noted that my route gradually fell, then rose again beyond Axylou, before dipping into the cool waters of the Mediterranean.

The home of Andreas and Magda Christofi is the first house in Elediou. With greetings as colourful as the flowering roses and dahlias that surrounded their courtyard, I was overwhelmed by their beautiful daughters hugging me, and sons, sisters and brother-in-laws shaking my hand. I stayed with them for an hour, my despondency lost in a whirlwind of hospitality.

I sat under a tubular frame that supported an enormous grapevine, some three metres overhead. This framework is often seen attached to Cypriot houses, for besides the vine producing a handsome crop of grapes, its foliage also shades the terrace from the summer heat. Magda rightly assumed I hadn't eaten that morning, as she and her daughters brought me plates of *koupepia*, *flaounes* and fruit. In these first few days I tasted more delicacies than I had ever done in my life. I did not, however, at any time sample *strouthos*!

Andreas had been *mukhtar* of his village for the past twenty two years. He was small and stocky; a good looking man with a mop of white hair and handlebar moustache. I was drinking my third glass of orange juice when, after a charming speech, he presented me with a cheque from the villagers of Elediou. As I journeyed on I would often recall a wonderful welcome like this, moments of kindness, or a fond farewell. They were pleasant and positive thoughts that pulled me through many difficult times. The warmth of Andreas and his family stayed with me a long time.

Somewhere to my right, on the upper slopes of the Ezousas valley, lay the old village sites of Eledio and Axylou. The latter, near the church of Agios Alexandros, is the reputed burial place of a small number of Cypriot saints. The present village was Turkish, with some of its renovated houses being used by refugees. I passed through without conversation. The only sign of life being a man across the street skewering mushrooms onto a spit, while his wife brandished a stick at their straying goats.

Yellow fingers of corn spread into the hillsides on the way to Nata, and the strange call of a francolin carried from the fields. I was drifting among a cloud of butterflies, watching the delicate and synchronized way of their flights and landings on favourite flowers. With the soul-destroying mountains and foothills behind me, I strolled down gentle slopes. The going was easy now... even pain had lost its bite. As I turned the bend near a limestone quarry I saw the ocean, and over a copse of trees the red-tiled roofs of Nata.

Near its entrance, jingling bells drew my attention to a

young man herding goats down the hillside. His flock settled in a grassy hollow nibbling at the trees. The shepherd sat smoking a cigarette watching my approach. He was Syrian, and insisted I join his two brothers for some refreshment. Ahmed directed me to the house, and minutes later I sat in the late afternoon sun eating bananas and sipping lemon tea on their front porch.

I was just preparing to leave when a heavy hand clamped down on my shoulder. Ahmed had returned. 'Please, you must eat,' he said. 'My brother cook very good!'

Not wishing to offend them I stayed, sharing strange but delicious mixtures of Syrian and Greek cuisine while listening to them reminisce about their beloved homeland. In 1815 an English traveller named William Turner had passed through this area, his privilege was to stumble upon the ruins of a Venetian church... mine had been to meet Ahmed and his brothers.

As Nata disappeared behind me, there was a noticeable change in the landscape. The dark earth turned to sandstone, and huge granite boulders edged the roadside. As the sun began to fall into the western hills I rested again. From Pentalia I'd walked almost thirty kilometres and my legs simply buckled under the strain.

Why I should stop in such an uncomfortable place I will never know, because I could only half sit and lean against the rocks. Perhaps Aphrodite herself was smiling upon me... for these rocks were my only protection when the dogs came.

I heard them first, barking and snapping at each other in the field below. Then suddenly they appeared over the ridge: four savage creatures in search of food... or blood! One was a pointer, the others cross-breeds - all of them abandoned and wild. Their coats were matted with oil and mud, and the pointer, last of the bunch up on to the road, was lame in its back leg. He lay there growling while the others approached me barking at a furious rate. I stood perfectly still. Two of the mongrels surged forward and then retreated as if testing me out, but the third was my real danger. A grey, wolf-like creature that seemed a cross between a husky and an alsation. He was less than four metres away, its bark turning to an ugly snarl as he crept nearer. I spoke quietly, trying to distract him while I reached for my pack.

The other two paced up and down menacingly, but there was no way behind me - my back protected by the rock face. They began to whine, and not knowing what to do returned to the pointer. Without taking my eyes from their leader, I now held my pack in front of me ready to fend him off. He had closed to two metres, the whites of his eyes red with anger. The hair stood vertical on its back, and my heart pounded as its bared teeth glistened razor sharp with saliva. My throat was dry and sweat trickled from my brow, knowing his bite could easily remove a chunk of flesh... my flesh! I watched him prowl, ever nearer...

The other dogs were barking now but they seemed distant... back in the fields. The mongrel was distracted. He backed away in a sudden fit of ferocious barking that almost stopped my heart with fright. Long after he'd gone I stood rooted to the spot, grateful that I was left in one piece. An hour later I was still looking over my shoulder.

Somewhere in the eastern valley near the river Xeros, lay the remains of Phinikas. To visit there would have meant negotiating a two hundred metre slope then clambering back to the road: an unnecessary hardship I could do without. It was a forsaken Turkish village, eliminated from my route by Phylactis and his father. At this stage I was not disappointed.

Having passed through barley fields and clusters of sugar cane, I crested a hill and sighted the Asprokremnos Dam, its waters lying deep and unruffled in the fading light. I was on the western side of the dam, and to walk its length would bring me to my last village of the day. A few kilometres on, I stopped at a sign welcoming me to Anarita. Somewhere in the village was an octopus. At five o'clock I began the search for its owner: an Englishman named John Orr.

CHAPTER 6

CHARLIE

Both streets and pavements were jammed with cars, scooters and pick-up trucks. Most had keys left in their ignition, literally abandoned in the rush for the best seats at the village festival. I had heard the tannoy system long before reaching the school, now it was deafening... the announcer shouting herself hoarse down a microphone at the excitement of an egg and spoon race. I passed them by as quickly as I could. I'd been shot at, almost made into a dog's dinner, now my eardrums were in danger of being shattered. Fortunately, I retreated in the general direction of John's residence.

It was one of several houses occupied by people like myself, who had retired to live in Cyprus, or otherwise purchased as a holiday home. I recognized his garden from Dorathy's description, its crazy-paved areas weaving between a mass of colourful shrubs and plants up to a shaded terrace. John greeted me at the door.

He was a man in his sixties, frail at the time as he was just recovering from a bout of pneumonia. But his eyes had lost the dark, languid signs of the illness, and he spoke with the passion and quiet confidence of a learned man. His guest, by contrast, I found rather pretentious. A man who strongly advised me to give up the walk, implying that because of my injuries mine was now a lost cause. It was difficult suppressing a yawn in his company before John tactfully suggested I might like to see my room and freshen up.

The house was very spacious, with an open-plan design downstairs and several rooms occupying the two upper-levels. Refreshed by a long cool shower, and with his friend departing soon afterwards, John and I sat talking over a beer. He possessed the kind of knowledge that one finds fascinating to listen to, especially when I enquired about his unusual hobby.

'Oh, let's eat first of all, shall we?' he said, modestly. 'I thought we'd dine out at a local taverna, if that's alright?'

I nodded. 'Sure... that's fine by me.' I thought it impolite to refuse - even though this would be my third cooked meal of the day!

'I'll tell you all about it when we get back.' We climbed into his car. 'You can meet Charlie as well.'

'Charlie?'

'Yes,' he smiled. 'My pet octopus!'

Apart from being an excellent photographer, John's main hobby was malacology: the study of molluscs. He collected specimens from all over the world, and until his recent illness had still dived for them, mainly off the Cyprus coast. John retained their shells, and his collection, meticulously sectioned in drawers and display cabinets, is unique on the island. It was on such a trip around the Paphos coastline that he found Charlie, and upon our return to the house John told me about him.

'He was only a tiny thing,' he motioned with his fingers. 'About the size of an old penny washed up in a rock pool.'

'Has he grown much?' I asked.

'Well, lets go up,' John replied, leading the way. 'He must be hungry by now, and hopefully he'll come out of his cave.'

On the top floor we entered his study. The room was filled with technical equipment, microscopes, cameras, books and water containers. There was a long tank which was Charlie's home, and smaller one's nearby, containing limpets... Charlie's food supply. I looked inside but saw nothing.

'He's in the cave... Come on, Charlie, we have a visitor.' John tapped the glass with his knuckle. Nothing stirred. 'I spent hours building him a nice cave,' he said, fishing out a limpet for his pet, 'and by morning he'd wrecked it! I tried again with the same result, then left him to it for a while. He's built this one himself.'

I peered in again - and this time I saw him... not Charlie, exactly, just an evil looking eye watching me. John had the limpet on a long silver spoon which he lowered into the tank and held it away from the cave's entrance. He called again: 'Come out, Charlie. I know you're...' Long tentacles wavered upwards towards the spoon and grabbed the limpet.

‘How does he eat it?’

‘Oh, he sucks the thing then spits out its shell… I’ll try again. He might come out this time.’ He repeated the process and Charlie emerged, his body now grown to the size of a large teacup. John would keep him, he said, until he was big enough to safely return to the sea and fend for himself.

I had heard of people being born with a silver spoon in their mouths… but never an octopus! I only hoped Charlie would make it.

My next morning proved to be a late start. John had made a breakfast of mangoes, boiled eggs and bread and butter, with two hot mugs of tea. It was difficult to muster the energy to leave, but as we said good-bye I felt in high spirits at the thought of a day’s easier terrain. I began to stroll the fields of rustling corn, moving on towards Timi.

Some thirty-five years earlier, a government survey suggested that a mixture of more than five hundred Greek and Turkish people resided there. But passing through, I saw only dogs chasing schoolboys on noisy scooters, and two old-timers asleep on coffee-shop chairs. There was a small Christian church, apparently one of several on the island used as a mosque when Cyprus fell to the Ottoman Turks in 1570, but little else to savour in the heat. I forked left outside the village to meet the thunder of traffic back on the main highway. My route had almost turned a full circle. At the sign to Paphos International Airport I was now barely sixteen kilometres west of my starting point at Petra tou Romiou.

Mandria was much smaller, and in its entirety, the only village lying south of the coast road between the Limassol border and Kato Paphos. Its entrance was lined with mature pine trees, whose trunks were whitewashed, I presumed, to signify their presence in vehicles' headlights. Cypriots are not the best drivers in the world... so it was a wise precaution.

Close to the sea beyond Mandria lies an ancient quarry, its sides pierced by vaulted tunnels in an area said to have once held a Latin convent. A marble capital and female head, reputed to be from the site, can be seen above the west door of Mandria's church. My friends in the coffee-shop defended this, however, saying it was from Agios Arkona, a chapel further west. They insisted I write it down with great clarity.

Along these southern shores the open fields are rich fertile plains that yield significant fruit and vegetable crops for the surrounding villages. Slicing through them is the main highway, and soon, vast concrete stilts supporting a planned motorway extension will vandalize both land and sky. Unlike the great Asprokremnos Dam, concealed in the bosom of gentle hills, it cannot be a welcome sight for the villagers. For me, crossing this dam would save time and energy, and knowing there were sheltering trees in its vicinity I plodded on, happy to be away from the choking traffic fumes.

Back at John's house in Anarita, the barometer had shown eighteen degrees centigrade under his covered terrace; now at mid-day, the heat was stifling. My breathing became laboured, and I encountered great difficulty in reaching the dam. I assumed these plains would be easy walking, but with the low altitude and unforgiving sun

Coffee-shop (cafenion) friends

comes humidity. The air was dry and lifeless, sending rivers of perspiration down my back as I finally approached the enormous walls of the dam.

An informative sign told me the Asprokremnos was an earth dam of English design, constructed over a four year period between 1978 - 82. Its reservoir area covers two and a half square kilometres, with a capacity of fifty-one million cubic metres. An irrigation project, completed a year after the dam by French and English contractors, has fourteen pumping stations supplying water through forty-one kilometres of main pipelines to the local community. It is also one of six reservoirs in the region stocked with a wide variety of fish.

Below me, a dozen anglers sat in silent dedication with their eyes glued to the still waters, completely unaware of the laden figure trundling across their horizon. At the far side of the dam I found a cool shelter of carob trees. The rations in my pack allowed for an apple and water lunch-break. It was a pleasant spot with view of the road I was heading for. I stayed for almost an hour.

No-one passed by except an occasional bird, the finest of which being a golden oriele. Like me, he was a migrant without his soul mate... returning to the island every year, but now seemingly out of his normal territory. Its bright yellow body and black wings flashed north-east towards the Troodos range, where they raise their young in the high branches of plane trees. I watched him out of sight before nestling down myself into a mini siesta.

As the ocean disappeared behind me, the plains began to rise to a distant hill. There, with its church sparkling like a diamond in the clear blue sky, I could see Choletria. The occupants had been re-housed some two hundred metres higher than the old village in the Xeros valley. But as so often happens at this time of day, all was quiet when I roamed the streets.

I entered a coffee-shop to find its owner, an old lady dressed in black, cat-napping in a chair. Next to her was a small refrigerator, and as quietly as I could I removed a can of lemonade and sat nearby. Her kind face was etched with wrinkles and crowned by a plain head scarf. She wore a thick cardigan over her long skirt, with woolly stockings encased in calf-length boots. Her dainty hands lay clasped over her bosom, moving only to the gentle rhythm of her breathing. Apart from this, she looked unnervingly dead... never flickering an eyelid as I placed my money on a tray beside her and left.

Sandstone soil began to redden the fields and banks of daisies tumbled into the roadway as I climbed towards Stavrokono. My legs had taken the strain well from Choletria. I'd managed five kilometres without a stop, but tired of the sun I needed to rest. The village was Turkish and seemingly deserted, yet as I sat in the doorway of an empty house I heard the sound of a child's laughter.

A young couple were playing with their daughter in the garden as I approached, and without hesitation they invited me to join them for some refreshment. Stelios and Lisa were refugees from the north, who had lost their home in Morphou during the invasion. They, along with twenty other refugees, now occupied Stavrokonos.

'It's peaceful, and we are happy here,' Stelios told me.

But his longing was all too clear when he spoke of Morphou. Like hundreds of others he waits in the hope that one day they can return to the north... and home.

We talked about many things, and when the time came to leave, Lisa insisted on a parcel of cake, fruit and a can of beer for my journey. The sun was casting long shadows in the street when Stelios walked me to the edge of his adopted village. He offered his hand, wishing me well as we parted. Here was a man whose world had been destroyed - but not his heart. I admired his courage.

Throughout the journey I had used a system when climbing. It not only eased the pain in my legs but also assisted my breathing difficulties. I walked in measured paces: fifty, a hundred, one hundred and fifty... and so on; each punctuated with a rest depending on the severity of an incline. On the road to Kelokedara my pace had fallen to one hundred. I had eaten an apple since breakfast, so perched on a high ridge I tucked into Lisa's food parcel to help my fatigue. With the sun's fading warmth on my shoulders, I watched a flock of birds gliding across the Diarizos valley. The next day I would follow its river for the last time back to the sea.

My map showed an abundance of vineyards on the eastern slopes, and north-west, the remains of a Late Byzantine church, Panagia Sindi, one of several churches and monasteries isolated in the depths of a valley. I could only surmise that this was because of access to water and fertile earth along the riverbanks, but no doubt the monks had a more profound reason for building there. I made notes - yet never discovered their motives.

Onward, and struggling at a pace of fifty, I was relieved

to find a standpipe where I stripped to the waist and drenched myself from head to toe in cold water. After that, nothing felt better than rounding that last bend to see my final village of the day - and suddenly, there it was. Kelokedara lay in a hollow, and beyond, the fading sun slowly cast its shadows over the mountains. I watched in awe as the colour drained away from the forests... their greenery turning dark as a raven's wing. From Anarita, I had climbed six hundred metres. My legs were sore but not painful, and I whistled cheerfully as the smell of roses and orange blossom floated to me on the breeze.

I was introduced to the *mukhtar* by Petros, a young man who had earlier made a touching speech offering me the freedom of Kelokedara. 'You sleep anywhere you like in the village,' he assured me. 'But our *mukhtar* has very nice house. Come...'

Adonis smiled in agreement to Petros' suggestion when he greeted me in his little shop. He insisted on carrying my pack, and as we set off down a steep road a voice roared from an upstairs window.

'Hey, English! Where are you from... Birmingham?'

I looked up into the white-whiskered face of an old man in striped pyjamas. 'Yes. Well, near to Birmingham,' I replied.

'Poli kala!' he shouted. 'I have friend, Yiannis... er, John Summers. We were together in Crete... The army. You understand?' Barely a pause, and then... 'Why do you limp? Are you hurt?'

I nodded once to all three questions.

'He lives in Birmingham now,' he continued. 'You must know him, my friend?'

'I'm afraid I...'

'Wait!.. I have photograph, please.'

Adonis spoke to him in Greek, saying I was tired and needed rest. The old man raised his hand to apologize. '*Signomi. Endaxi*... OK,' he nodded. '*Avrio* he come to my house. Plenty to eat... Plenty whisky, eh? *Endaxi*?'

The *mukhtar* nodded, smiling broadly. '*Ne. Ne. Avrio*! *Avrio*!'

I waved, wishing him goodnight, but before closing his shutters with a bang he leaned precariously out of the window giving me a thumbs-up sign, saying, 'English good... Very good!'

My room was in keeping with the remainder of the *mukhtar's* house: freshly painted doors and cupboards, with the white stone walls as spotless as the floor. Across the courtyard was a toilet and bathroom . I shaved and showered in the comfort of hot water until roused by a knock at the door. It was Adonis to say I was wanted on the telephone.

It's always moments like this when an unsettling feeling churns your stomach... panic! Who on earth can it be? No-one in the world knows I'm staying here. I've lost contact with my charity team - so who? My wife? Some-one's ill back home, or... I picked up the phone, my heart pounding. 'Hello?'

'Meester Petros?'

'Yes?.. speaking.'

'Aah! We find you at last! This is the Chief of Police in Paphos. How are you, my friend? You are still walking?'

'Yes. I...'

'Bravo! We thought you were dead!' A loud bellow of laughter, then... 'Your friends at the hospital, they worry, so my officers from Kouklia have search for you.'

'Er... Well, I'm fine. But how did... ?'

'Poli kala!'... followed by another chuckle. 'A man saw you at Kholetria. So we know Petros OK. *Endaxi*?'

'Endaxi. And thank you for...'

'You're welcome,' he said. The phone clicked, and just as briskly he was gone.

Emilianou ushered me to her table. She ate very little, her satisfaction being in the sight of Adonis and I devouring *koupepia, sikoti, patates, bizelia* and a salad with olives and *halloumi* cheese, together with yoghurt and thick slices of bread. It was a perfect end to my first week on the road. I fell into bed around ten-thirty thoroughly knackered.

The sun rose on the way to Trachypedoula, its beams

lighting the Diarizos river and waking the whole valley. My track wriggled eastwards, taking me to the village by eight o'clock. This was normally a good time to find some company at the *cafenion*, but no-one stirred except the owner. His smile lit up the doorway, asking me to join him for coffee.

'*Ne... Metrios, parakalo*.' I asked for medium.

'*Endaxi... Ela! Ela*! Sit down.' He manoeuvred two chairs beside a table and I watched him prepare my drink.

With local coffee, the sugar is added to the water and coffee before heating - so it is ordered by taste: *'glikos'* - *'metrios'* or *'sketos'*. He mixed one heaped teaspoonful of finely ground coffee beans with the desired quantity of cold water and sugar into an *embriki*: a small, individual-sized pot with a long handle. Aristos then held the *embriki* over the gas until the coffee boiled, forming a creamy froth called *'kaimaki'*. He weaved his way between the tables and chairs, serving it piping hot with a customary glass of cold water on a tray.

We hardly had chance to speak before Aristos was brewing again as a few more customers arrived. They were sweat-stained and dusty from working the land. I joined them outside, enjoying the coolness of shade and the smell of coriander drifting from the fields. This is a medicinal plant, one of them told me, taken as an aid to digestion. The fruits are used in cooking, and their oil for perfume-making and the distilling process of gin and kirsch. I was becoming more educated by the minute.

The men were absorbed in my maps, showing great interest in the 'donation book' I produced. They generously collected fifty pounds then, after helping me on with my pack, directed me to a path I needed outside the village.

I passed through gardens of giant artichokes and prickly pears before chatting to a teacher near the village school. He assured me my path lay just ahead, but no-one used it anymore. I soon found out the reason why. Its steepness, together with a surface of loose stones and rocks, meant I descended most of the time sideways. My knee quickly objected to such harsh treatment, and before long the pain returned with a vengeance. A hardship made worse by the constant buzzing and torment from swarms of green-bodied flies.

The path was murderous... and I suffered for it. But with two thirds of my journey to go, there was no use dwelling on mistakes. I would rest the night in Kouklia, then see about visiting the hospital from there.

With my back to the sun I walked the valley. Below the road ran the Diarizos river, and somewhere beyond, the locked monastery where I had planned my first night's shelter. It was easy going from here, and I soon approached Agios Georgios. The village held no more than twenty properties which, along with their neighbours, seemed rich in arable land. The river disappeared into meadows flushed with orange and lemon groves that spread south into the vegetable fields of Mamonia. A place where John de Dampierre, Constable of Cyprus, had died in 1308.

At a roadside taverna a lady gave me orange juice and ten pounds from her till for the charity fund. I whiled away my time watching swallows dive to and from a nest in the sloping rafters above my head. Woven against the end of a fluorescent tube light, it attracted conversation with the arrival of some English tourists, who also chipped in with a donation.

These spontaneous gifts were most rewarding, as they made amends for the disappointing response in some of the larger, well-populated villages. Whenever I moved away from the remote pathways, someone would recognize me on the open road. People in cars or villagers in their pick-up trucks would stop for a friendly chat, some gladly offering money. Their kind words were always a boost to flagging moral.

At Fasoula, I entered the fenced perimeter of a Turkish mosque to shelter from the sun. Though rotting facia boards hung from the roof, its walls were sound. The minaret was also intact, and sitting in its shade one could imagine this tiny village echoing with the voice of a muezzin calling Muslims to prayer from the tower's balcony. But no more... its houses and land had perished - the earth scorched barren by unrelenting heat and years of neglect.

A few kilometres south I crossed the river, thankful for its cool waters filling my boots. I wandered aimlessly between the hollow dwellings of Souskiou, a ghost-like village without any visible sign of its past. In another twenty years the sweat and tears that saw its creation would be no more than dust and stones scattered on a hillside. The main road was a more comforting sight - except for the sun, which offered no mercies other than a shaded almond tree. I rested here, picking a handful of unripened nuts to eat.

Along with the carob and olive, almond trees are commonly found on these lower hill slopes and plains. The nuts may be eaten in their mature or green form; in this raw state the shells were soft and very tasty. I knew that almonds were also processed as a sweet drink, called Soumada... but I settled for water. This was my first meal of the day and it put me in a spirited mood heading for Nikoklia.

I had read that in ancient times travellers were most impolite in their reference towards the Cypriot people. By the seventeenth century, however, Lithgow reported they were '... of great civility, hospitable to their neighbours and exceedingly affectionate to strangers'. His observations were apparent in the greeting I received from a young woman strolling in the village.

At the *mukhtar's* house she invited me in, wiping clean her table and offering me cake, fruit and orange juice. I asked of the *mukhtar*... and wished I hadn't. Her voice fell to a whisper as she explained that he had recently died in a freak accident, leaving her with four young children. She was proud, she said, when the village honoured his name by electing her to continue his duties as *mukhtar*. I humbly accepted her gift of thirty pounds for the charity.

Nikoklia was reputed to be named after Nicocles, King of Paphos, c320 BC. If my studies were true, it boasted a church - dated 1768 - that contained several contemporary icons. There also lay a marble Corinthian capital and column near the church which, in all probability, had come from an ancient city that once stood on the east side of the Diarizos river.

Although refreshed, I politely declined to visit the old

church - my goal before darkness fell was to reach Kouklia. For here lay the remnants of Palaepaphos... and the site of Aphrodite's temple.

CHAPTER 7

APHRODITE'S TEMPLE

The ancient kingdom of Palaepaphos had once occupied a limestone plateau near the sea: an extensive area that was far greater than the present-day site known as Kouklia. The village came into view as I crested a hill from the river. Numerous excavations over the years have revealed that the old city was densely populated from the Archaic period to early Hellenistic times. But now it had diminished to a village where even I was known. I had lived there for a while three years earlier, and although changes were apparent, it would never attain its former glory.

On my left, a series of tarmac roads earmarked a new area to accommodate villagers whose existing homes were under threat from further archaeological research. Their stone-built houses smother and preserve fragments of the ancient city. A retired curator of the temple's museum once told me that if funds were available, untold historical treasures could still be found. I was looking forward to meeting Georgios again that night. He was an interesting man.

A rest day was due in Kouklia, and all things considered,

I was particularly pleased to have made it to the village. I was on schedule, but even so, with my legs causing continual problems I had spent far too much time on the road. My progress had slowed dramatically. I had now carried the injuries for several days - my visit to the hospital was long overdue.

I walked into Kouklia police station... not to give myself up - but to thank the officers for proving to their chief I was still alive! They, however, like the man on the road to Archimandrita, thought it was an impossible venture. Nevertheless, they still plied me with coffee and biscuits and wished me well. It was growing dusk when I reached my accommodation.

Yiannis and Androula had invited me to stay in an annexe of apartments adjoining their house. I knew them well; they were a hard-working family. While Yiannis tended the land, Androula spent most days running their village supermarket. In the evenings you would probably find them both cooking and serving in their popular taverna, 'The Leda'.

Words at the coffee-shop had already signalled my presence in Kouklia. I had washed my trousers and was pegging them out on the line when Georgios, the old curator, arrived. He was closely followed by Costas, the village Romeo - who was in his eighties.

Georgios was born in Kouklia in 1919. He had been a prisoner of the Germans for six years, captured at Kalamata in Greece, before taking up his appointment as a custodian with the Department of Antiquities in 1946. A position he held for thirty-three years. We sat under a beautiful starlit sky, Georgios smartly dressed in a dark suit and opened necked shirt... and me in tartan pyjamas. I always found him to be a kind man, very polite. When he spoke his voice was distant, subdued perhaps, by sixty years of cigarette smoke. I asked him if he remembered Aphrodite's temple as a boy.

'Oh, yes. But there were only stones then,' he whispered. 'Some of the temple ruins had been excavated in 1888 by the Cyprus Exploration Fund, but when I was a boy a lot of Turkish people lived here, and many of the villagers used stones from the site to fix their houses. It was years later... 1950, I believe, before any modern archaeological research took place.'

'You were the curator then, Georgios. It must have been an interesting time?'

He smiled. His memory stirred by my question. *'Ne... Ne.* I worked with clever, experienced men from England, Germany and Switzerland... All over. Very good archaeologists who have found many wonderful pieces of Paphos history.'

I asked him if he recalled meeting the distinguished writer, Colin Thuberon, who had mentioned Georgios in his book, 'Journey into Cyprus'.

'No,' he replied, dryly.

'But Georgios, you're a celebrity. Not many people have entertained a famous writer in their house.'

He shrugged in typical Cypriot manner. 'Me?.. No! I don't remember such things. Only my work.'

Georgios was a modest man. I remember his dedication being acknowledged in a local newspaper by the eminent German archaeologist F.G.Maier. Georgios had been sharp enough one day to notice some young boys in the village firing bits of stone from their catapults. He chastised, but later thanked them for showing him the spot where their 'ammunition' had originated. Those fragments of stone he recognized as tesserae, and after informing the Department of Antiquities, an excavation of the area in 1972 revealed an almost perfect mosaic of Leda and the Swan. It has been attributed to the late second century A.D., and although the floor was left at the site, its central panel is now exhibited in the Archaeological Museum in Nicosia. The existing mosaic, which lies north-west of the temple, is a replica. No doubt this was the reason Yiannis, Georgios' son, had so named his taverna.

Any further discussions of historical interest, however, were soon disrupted by the back-slapping I received at the arrival of Costas.

He was a mischievous, but likeable rogue. Much older than Georgios, yet still nimble enough to career around the village on a scooter. I had become his friend through averting a coffee-shop brawl in 1992 over a game of cards.

There were three of them playing: Costas, Panis, the village violinist and Costas' brother - whose name I could never remember... or even pronounce. Strong words were exchanged, in which I gathered from the smirk beneath Costas' handlebar moustache, that he was not only winning... but cheating. It was meant to be a 'friendly' game - no money involved - but honour was most certainly at stake. The table went over... Costas, grabbed by the throat, cast an appealing glance of innocence at me as his older brother pounced, his clenched fist ready to strike. I managed to part them, and rescue poor old Panis who was buried under the table and a pile of chairs.

Costas was reminiscing about it now. I was laughing, Georgios barely smiled his amusement. He had heard it so often before. By the time they left, my soaking wet trousers had almost dried in the warm night air. As usual, I slept very soundly.

Dorathy arrived in Kouklia at ten-thirty the next morning and drove me to Paphos General Hospital, where Phylactis immediately ushered me in to see his orthopaedic surgeon. The crepe bandage was removed from my right shin, and the surgeon determined the swelling either side of my tibia as tendonitis - more commonly referred to as shin splints. But the left knee was a more painful diagnosis. My leg being twisted and turned in every direction, until finally - when I'd descended from the ceiling - the verdict was a rupture of the medial meniscus.

At that moment I felt the prospect of continuing the walk extremely doubtful. I left hospital walking like a Frankenstein mummy. My right leg strapped from ankle to knee, and my left bandaged from calf to thigh. The doctor had prescribed cream to reduce inflammation and a supply of strong painkillers, but advised that only rest, then further treatment to re-build the muscles above the knee. Later, I discovered these tissue fibres had wasted away by four centimetres.

I rested at Yiannis and Androula's apartment until late afternoon, doing nothing more strenuous than to study

Panis - violinist of Kouklia

the terrain I had yet to cross... and willing myself to continue. On a brighter note, came news from the charity that an encouraging amount of money had been coming in from the villages. At five o'clock I ventured back towards the river to call upon some English friends who had once been my neighbours in Kouklia. Ruth and Ken insisted I stayed for tea, and also presented me with seventy-five pounds which they had kindly collected from the English residents. This most welcomed contribution eventually made the village donation into a respectable sum.

Whilst living in Kouklia, I visited the site of Aphrodite's temple many times, but a place I had never seen was the north-east gate of the old city. It occupied a commanding position on Marcello Hill, located about seven hundred metres from the apartment. Outside the city walls archaeologists discovered the important remains of a siege ramp, constructed by the Persians when they attacked Palaepaphos in 498 B.C. The light was fading when I put my legs to the test over the rough ground.

I made it to the site in twenty minutes, my only companion being the distant silhouette of a shepherd boy herding goats. In the stillness, the sound of his crook swishing through the parched grass echoed across the fields. A cluster of stars were gathering, and a silver jet-plane banked and glided in from the sea towards Paphos airport.

It is difficult to comprehend ancient ruins. To a layman like me they are merely a pile of stones - but here, even though reconstructed in places, the siege and defensive structures form a graphic illustration of ancient warfare. The original city walls were over six metres thick, protected further by a perimeter ditch ten metres wide and four metres deep. Its north-east gate was also a formidable structure, which had a twelve metre thoroughfare flanked by huge bastions.

On their advance, it is thought the Persian army destroyed a sanctuary, using columns, alters and sculptures, together with soil and tree branches to build the siege mound, thus elevating their wooden towers to scale the wall. Hundreds of bronze and iron arrowheads were excavated from the ramp, along with spear points and bronze helmets, proving a vicious battle had raged to protect the city. In the semi-darkness I could make out the tunnels designed by the Greeks to counter this attack. Bronze cauldrons were found in the shafts, said to be used to fire the wooden contents of the mound, thereby causing subsidence and the collapse of Persian towers.

The sky was ablaze with stars as I returned to the village, remembering as I did that the Persian army had, after all, been victorious. Records of the historian, Herodotus, reveal the final capture of all Greek cities. Long after these fortifications collapsed, the Romans built a road there. It ran beyond Archimandrita to the villages I had previously trekked through, higher up the Diarizos valley.

At five-thirty the next morning, I left the slumbering village in the hope of finding a light traffic-flow down on the main highway. But the aesthetic lure of Aphrodite's temple in the hour before dawn is irresistible. I left my pack by the entrance, and clambered over the gate.

In their quest for a meaningful life, the hopes, fears and

emotions of a community were expressed through myth and legend. Procured and re-created in sacred rituals, they have carried many ideals and historical situations through generations of uncertainty. Despite being fought and conquered by untold nations, the island's fame was not born from economic or political power, but rested within the stone pillars of Aphrodite's sanctuary. This was her most famous shrine in antiquity.

The Classical writers - as in their diverse references to Aphrodite - also presented a variety of theories on the temple's origins. The legend from Tacitus attributes its foundation to Kiniras, the wealthy Cypriot king, and father of Adonis. While Pausanias maintained that the sanctuary was built by the Arcadian king, Agapinor, whose ship was cast onto the shores of Paphos during a storm. But Herodotus followed the tradition that Phoenicians founded Aphrodite's temple. In truth, perhaps we will never know.

After many years of archaeological study, however, signs that her temple existed here are unquestionable. The reverse side of Roman coins in the Cyprus Museum are testimony to its architecture. From Augustus to the Severans, these coins carried the fame of Aphrodite throughout the whole Imperium. In all but slight variation, they show identical structural detail. The temple is depicted as a triparte building with a fenced courtyard in front. Its central area featuring a conical object flanked by free-standing pillars, topped by horns of consecration.

The Goddess of Love had cast aside her modesty by entertaining lovers. Among them was the god Mars, who in his jealousy of others, rode a horse-drawn chariot into the mountains and defeated the gryphons sent by God to protect the hill of jasper. He tore away a huge stone and set it down for Aphrodite's bed to subdue her passion. Hence, they placed not an effigy in her temple... but a rude unpolished block of jasper. This was yet another legendary tale of why the beauty of Aphrodite had simply turned into stone.

It was said in the days of Jesus that many Cypriot merchants travelled to Syria, and moved by his preachings begged him to return with them and shower his blessings on the people of Cyprus. But Jesus said he must first suffer the cross and die. Fearing his body may be disposed of, they entered the temple of Aphrodite and removed the conical stone, shaping therein a tomb for the Lord. Even when they heard of Jesus' death and burial the Cypriots preserved the tomb... for it would not be right that Aphrodite's image be likened to the sepulchre of Christ.

An array of sculptures came from the temple: statues of emperors and members of the Imperial House, proconsuls of the island, and dedications from merchants and Romans at Paphos - all signify by their inscriptions, Aphrodite's importance in Roman times. They are from an era which was possibly the richest in Imperial portrait sculpture in Cyprus. But the rare fabric that survived from antiquity was lost during the construction of a sugar cane refinery in the fourteenth century. This adjoined the Lusignan Manor House, thereby condemning the temple ruins into a quarry.

The sun had not yet risen, but its warmth had begun to stir the cobwebs of mist on a mosaic floor. I traced my hand over its intricate patterns and the fragments of tesserae glistened... a myriad of colours sprang to life. It was an eerie, yet remarkable feeling to reach back in time; to realize that some two thousand years ago a Roman hand must have touched this very spot.

I returned to the village road, looking back at the Katholiki Church where some stone-etched inscriptions from the temple are built into its walls. Above its ruined cloisters the sky was streaked crimson and orange. I turned my back to the sun's arc as it glinted over the hills, and moved on past the east wing of the Chateau de Covacle. Its great cross-vaulted hall is probably the finest reminder of Frankish architecture in Cyprus.

I had travelled three kilometres west towards Paphos before the sun finally appeared over Kouklia. In ancient times, I would have faced hundreds of pilgrims and travellers on their way from the harbour in Nea Paphos to the temple. Worshippers came from every corner of the Roman world, and on festival days, crowned with myrtle and complemented by music, the procession would congregate at Aphrodite's shrine. My journey on this particular morning was rather more perilous.

Even at this early hour the density of traffic determined that my only way of survival was to walk a stony verge. The strip of tarmac was no more than six metres wide, its verge stretching barely a metre either side. Cars, lorries, coaches, high powered Izusu and Mitsubishi trucks and taxi's, all screamed past at death-provoking speeds. Nothing could venture across this road without being squashed to pulp. I literally walked through the dead and dying: hedgehogs, birds, the bodies of two cats, one of which was still twitching in the throes of death. It was no place for animals or walkers... it wasn't meant to be.

I was the trespasser. I could not expect drivers to give way, as the highway was far too narrow for courtesy to pedestrians. I always disliked these roads, avoiding them at every opportunity, but at times there was simply no alternative. It was, therefore, a great relief to reach my next village.

Acheleia was chief of the five bailiwicks into which the district of Paphos was divided in the Lusignan period. It was a centre for the thriving sugar cane industry in those days, and according to local tradition it is said that buffalo used to swim across from Egypt to feed on the cane. In 1806, Ali Bey el Abbassi noted that some of the arches of an aqueduct, which had supplied the sugar works, were still intact among the ruins. I could neither deny or gain confirmation of these informative gems... there was no-one around to talk to. Instead, I picked up a track which led through an orange grove. It was time for breakfast.

Before starting out from Kouklia I had removed the strapping from my right leg, and having walked virtually non-stop for twelve kilometres I felt in good form. The sun was lost in a darkening sky, and for the first time there seemed a hint of rain. I was resting under a tree eating my second orange when a truck came around the corner and screeched to a halt in a plume of dust. A farmer had caught me red-handed eating his fruit.

Not since a boy had I experienced such guilt. 'Scrumping' - as we used to call it - was a practical answer to one of my mother's mouth-watering apple pies. No questions asked; no recriminations made, scrumping was a much more subtle word than stealing... and only used where 'misplaced' fruit was concerned. But the secret was never to get caught, yet in spite of my past astuteness, here I was nabbed... good and proper.

I rose awkwardly, my embarrassment quite apparent. The farmer stepped from his truck. He was a tall wiry man, dressed in a blue open-necked shirt, faded jeans and thick-soled boots... the kind you wouldn't relish being aimed at your backside! His eyes shone like black marble, and held a smile of recognition. 'You are the walker, eh?'

'Yes. I... I was hungry. I'm afraid I...'

'No problem,' he laughed. 'Please take. Help yourself, my friend. Take more for your journey.'

I breathed a sigh of relief, and more out of thanks than uncertainty, asked him to show me the road to Agia Varvara.

On his way from the more northern village of Nata, William Turner arrived in Agia Varvara to find that all of its residents had perished in the plague. Many years before, a Turkish vessel foundered off the Paphos coast; its survivors took refuge on the island and the disease began to spread. It was said that twenty-two thousand people died. This Agia Varvara was a tiny village - alive and well - and as with most small or remote places, when company could be found I was always made welcome. A lady tending her goats bid me to join her. She brought a chair from the house, then a glass of lemonade on a lovely engraved silver tray. I sat among her chickens and flower pots mopping my brow. She gestured to my skinny frame, and giving me a toothless smile, produced an open-bladed knife from her apron and went back to the kitchen.

When she returned, the old lady was clutching a lump of stale bread. Holding it to her bosom she proceeded to hack off a thick slice while the chickens fought for crumbs. She placed it down, making the tray ring out... As it did so, there was another smile - straight from the heart this time. How could I refuse to eat it?

The *mukhtar*, I understood, was out on his tractor until noon, but the lady promised to tell him of my visit. By the time I had back-tracked to the main highway, a drizzle of rain began to fall. The traffic had reached a crescendo now, so close to my shoulder that lorries and coaches threatened to suck me under their wheels. The handkerchief I held to my face was little protection from the dust and choking fumes. I took shelter in Koloni, where the road divided a scattering of houses that led me on to Geroskipos.

The village was busy; its famous church and the shop-factories producing sweet Cyprus delight, were packed with tourists. It was a little early for lunch, but feeling tired and hungry I sat in a restaurant near the church and ordered half a chicken, with salad. Because of an early start that morning I spent a long time over my meal, writing postcards for home, then contacting the charity to let them know all was well. Suddenly the restaurant began to fill with people as thunder rolled in from the sea and driving rain sent them scurrying for cover. When the storm had passed I made my way to the church, determined this time to gain entrance by finding the caretaker. He was not working in his tiny cobblers shop, however, but in the church itself, surrounded by a group of Americans. I wandered around, unnoticed.

The church of Agia Paraskevi was built in the ninth century; its frescoes depict various bible scenes, and although very few of the Byzantine originals remain, some later works survive. Among them are: 'The Birth of Christ', 'The Raising of Lazarus from the Dead', The Betrayal', 'The Crucifiction' - and a rare scene representing 'The Baptism of Christ'. The five-domed church also held a fifteenth century icon, said to be found by a peasant near the sea, and revered as one of the rarest icons in Cyprus. There was a wonderful Sepulchre Relief from Russia, and a finely carved *iconostasi*. But apart from this splendour, a somewhat insignificant remark from the curator caught my attention. He was addressing his visitors regarding the south-western corner of the church... 'and some distance away' he was saying, 'was the entrance to a large cave which we believe to have been associated with the worship of Aphrodite.'

'Excuse me?' I interrupted. 'Do any signs of the cave remain?'

I was at the edge of the group now, and the old man turned, eyeing me over his spectacles. 'No. I'm afraid it was sealed about forty years ago. There's nothing...' He smiled, his voice trailing away as another question came from one of the Americans. I returned to the restaurant for a drink, the old man's words prompting me to check my notes. Ironically, they revealed the following...

'The whole area of Geroskipos was covered with trees and carpets of flowers in antiquity. On their way to the temple of Aphrodite, the pilgrims would visit here to offer sacrifices. In the churchyard of Agia Paraskevi the ruins of numerous columns and capitals were found, reaffirming reports from early travellers that the church was built on the foundations of a sanctuary.'

‘On his continuous journey through Acheleia, Ali Bey el Abbassi observed the Garden of Venus as a considerable plain that stretched along the seashore. The garden was in a ravine, filled with colourful flowers and a stream which seemed to originate from a large cave.’

‘This cave was also referred to in 1875 by General Di Cesnola, the American Consul in Cyprus. His researches at Kouklia had proved unprofitable and, travelling by donkey to Nea Paphos, he was captivated by a cave seemingly hewn out of solid rock. He recorded that it was an area of great beauty. Surrounded by the rich foliage of carob and olive trees, the cavern was gently filled by a stream which then trickled downwards to water neighbouring fields.’

In their text, and indeed to other learned travellers and historians, this was recognized as the original ‘Baths of Aphrodite’. It was a fascinating comparison.

By not consulting my maps, I made the error of completely missing the village of Agia Marinouda. I found myself instead, on a track that promised to lead me to Konia. My progress along these flatter plains had been steady, and with this short cut saving me a big detour, I breezed along. But like hundreds of pathways in the region, they can turn out as mere goat tracks that wander into a field... just like this one. I was surrounded by animals: pigs, chickens, goats, two donkeys and even a cow mooed its disapproval at my presence. The good news from my compass reading told me the direction was fine, providing I scaled a fifteen metre rock face at the end of the animal sheds. I looked around... there was no alternative.

I chose carefully, climbing the easiest section I could find. At the top I stood on a plateau that resembled a lunar landscape. Strange rock formations were riddled with holes like a giant sponge, with spiked shrubs sprouting like tufts of hair. It was difficult to walk on - and too easy to turn an ankle - so my progress was slow and tentative. I switched to the edge of the hilltop, trampling through some dead ferns where I could see the tarmac road to Konia a hundred metres ahead.

I had stopped to take a drink from my flask when I heard someone shouting in Greek. Below me was a builders yard where two men shovelled sand, while a third waved his arms frantically. Unaware of the horror in his face, I waved back. The two men stopped work and they too began shouting. They ran quite a distance towards me before I made out the word, *'fidi!' 'fidi!'...* and one man wriggled his hand like a serpent. It is one thing to assume there may be snakes around, but when someone tells you the place is alive with them, it gives you a whole new burst of energy... fright! It was the fastest I had moved for many a day. Half climbing - half sliding into the yard below, I was propelled down the rock face in seconds. The three men stood aghast at my agility. I thanked them, and after beating the dust from my trousers, accepted their kind offer of a Coca-Cola.

Konia was a sprawling village. I wandered around aimlessly for the *mukhtar* without success - not even a suggestion of his whereabouts. The most helpful person was a pretty young lady in a rose-filled garden, who promised to find him later and pass on my message. The afternoon was ending, and the sun burned with a final flourish as I reached the cross-roads to Armou. Back in the orange grove at Agia Varvara I had reduced the strapping on my leg, and although my knee was still swollen, the painkillers had been effective. But now, there was no rhythm to my stride. I was tiring fast, and all too frequently my boots scuffed the ground. At the cross-roads I had walked thirty kilometres.

The village houses were scattered over a steep hillside, yet fortune smiled in the form of a woman herding a few scraggy goats. She beckoned me to follow her up a narrow track, implying: 'Much better than the road. You follow, please. I know *mukhtar*, and his father's house.'

She was sprightly for her years and left me trailing behind, striding away agile as her goats. The animals annoyed her. They frequently stopped to feed from the leaves of overhanging trees, only to scamper on as the old lady tanked them with her long wooden staff. She led me to a pleasant house where I found Artemis, the *mukhtar*, sitting with his parents outside. At the edge of their garden my day's journey lay spread-eagled below. Through the hills, dying rays of sunlight trembled over Kouklia... and all that remained of Aphrodite's temple.

CHAPTER 8

OPPOSITES

Armou is one of several villages in Paphos favoured by English residents. With one exception, I was unfortunate enough to meet some of them. After being shown so much kindness by the Cypriot people, particularly the poor and needy, I was not prepared for such rudeness from my own compatriots. That night, I was to experience the cold, brusque attitude of the British. An 'US' and 'them' scenario; a side that illustrated perfectly... upper-class snobbery at its worst.

By comparison, Artemis and his parents Vassiliki and Christasos, welcomed me - a complete stranger and foreigner - into their home. I was allowed to shower and change my dusty clothes, which Vassiliki duly washed, they gave me food from their table and my own comfortable room to sleep in. The couple were so courteous, that later, on my return to their house with Artemis, I was initially reduced to an embarrassing silence. The situation was more unfortunate because Artemis assumed that generous donations would be made to the fund by his English neighbours. He was wrong.

Artemis was a big man, probably in his forties. He was smartly dressed in a blue shirt, dark suit and polished shoes... a real gent. The money he had given me from his Cypriot community was already very much appreciated, but he wanted to help even more. We were sharing a beer after our meal.

'Come, Petros. Drink up, eh? We collect something extra for the hospital.'

We climbed into his truck and began careering around the village to various points of call. Properties to which one associates money. Most were empty, or a movement in a curtain suggested so to unwelcome guests. Two in particular, answered their doors.

The first house, a huge rambling affair, did - after a considerable wait - answer the doorbell. A tall man opened the door marginally, looked at my clean but well-worn clothes, and prepared to close it again. He relented when Artemis came into view, making a weak joke to the *mukhtar* that he had already paid his village rates.

'No. I'm afraid it's me that's after your money this time,' I said, smiling. He looked on stony-faced as I explained that I was on a charity walk in aid of the General Hospital.

'We thought you might like to give money to help,' Artemis said, shuffling uneasily.

'Oh! Well... er... We have guests at the moment. We're rather tied up,' the man said.

I looked at him in disdain. He glanced once more at my

clothes, then with an impatient: 'Very well... Just wait there, will you?' he closed the door in our faces.

Had Artemis not been there I would have walked away. A few minutes passed before the door opened again and the man stood there holding out some money. 'There you go, *mukhtar*!' he cried in a jolly voice. 'We've had a collection for you.'

Artemis smiled, and I mumbled my thanks. The grand total from the man, his wife and honoured guests was three pounds!

At the second house I was actually invited to stand in the kitchen by a quietly-spoken husband. His wife, upon hearing our conversation, looked at me as though I was something to be scraped off a shoe. Artemis remained in the doorway. There followed an extraordinary investigation from the female occupant of the house into the why's and wherefore's of people collecting money for 'so-called good causes.' She was arrogant in her opinion of charities, and determined that she, nor her husband, would contribute except in extreme circumstances.

'I assure you, madam,' I finally interrupted. 'Walking seven hundred kilometres to help supply a piece of medical equipment that will save the lives of unborn babies is about as extreme as you can get!' I turned to leave in disgust, Artemis accepting the money from her husband. We had wasted twenty minutes for a miserly sum of two pounds. I had seen and heard enough, suggesting to Artemis that we call it a day. He seemed a glutton for punishment. We made one last call: a visit to the home of Chrissie Flint, a freelance journalist. At last... a welcome smile, a cup of tea and a little English sociability.

Artemis left me at his parents' house, and the next morning the couple stood proudly as I took their photograph. They were a nice family... some of their English neighbours would be enlightened by their hospitality and manners.

As usual, I was away bright and early, hooking my thumbs into the straps of my pack to ease the load. The clean morning air was always a joy, especially when you can saunter down a hill. At the cross-roads I saw the old lady again. She was still chastising her goats, but gave me a cheery wave as I walked the short distance to Marathounda.

The village was beginning to stir: chickens squawked and clucked in its narrow streets; a dog barked at my passing shadow; a man's sleepy voice called his son; window shutters squeaked open - a door slammed shut; birds sang and babies cried... and even on this warmest of days, there was a smell of burning wood. From an open doorway a sudden whoosh of water hit the street, spraying me in soapsuds. An old lady, blissfully unaware of my presence, shuffled back inside and closed the door. There was no activity at the village coffee-shop, so I returned once more to the main road, bearing east to Episkopi.

A series of ruined churches on this eastern side of Marathounda stretch southwards to the sea. Agia Mavri, Agios Mamas, Agia Marina, Agios Dhimitrianos and Agios Georgios lie in a particularly interesting formation. Whilst planning a route for my journey across this area, I observed there was a remarkable similarity in the churches' relativity to each other. A line passing through each location north to south revealed part of the pattern of stars

Shepherdess near Armou

known as the Plough - which in turn, represents the tail and hind quarters of the Great Bear in the Ursa Major constellation. I wondered if it was a coincidence that this constellation is associated with Zeus, king of the gods - and mythical father of Aphrodite? No doubt a comprehensive study would reveal more.

Episkopi lay on the west bank of the Ezousas river. It was a long trek over undulating landscape, with climbs that tore at the tendons of my shin again. Upon reaching the highest point, I sat at the roadside eating the cheese and tomato rolls Vassiliki had prepared for my journey. Below me, a yellow cornfield began to sway in the freshening breeze. Small clusters of wild flowers turned their faces to the sun, and scouring the land, a lonely magpie searched for its mate.

In the lowland areas I had seen an inordinate amount of solitary magpies. Although some regard it as bunkum, 'One for sorrow - two for joy' is a saying that still makes people uneasy at the sight of a lone magpie. As a boy, an old bird catcher once told me that when a magpie dies its chums and relatives gather to mourn its death, and help to find the remaining partner another mate. Intrigued, my friends and I would hide in gorse bushes on the high banks overlooking a field. There, we would sometimes watch dozens of magpies assemble; it was true they had strange rituals. The birds often wheeled into the air in tight circles a metre above the ground, or spread their wings and huddled together. This made fascinating black and white patterns which seemed to attract more of these extraordinary creatures from the air.

There was no such joy for my feathered friend. As I rose to continue my trek, it circled the field in vain... reminiscent of the Roman sculptor in his quest to create an image of Aphrodite.

'A model will not suffice,' he said. 'For no human possesses her perfection of body and soul; her sensuality, or purity. So flawless and unreachable is Aphrodite, that one may be forgiven for doubting her existence...'

The magpie also ended its search, flying away into the sun.

Where endless vineyards clad the rolling hills, my road dipped and twisted in pursuit. A mist shrouded the distant mountains, turning their enormity into no more than a pencil line tracing the sky. Three hours into my journey, a massive rock face overhung the road, climbing vertically at the village entrance to a church suspended on a high ledge.

It had proved a precarious site for a building. In 1953, an earthquake inflicted serious damage on the island, and this church, along with many others in the region, was razed to the ground. Indeed, the whole village had been under threat ever since. Seismic tests discovered a progressive land shift across an extensive area, and at one stage the Cyprus Government were planning to evacuate the whole village.

During my search for a property in Paphos a few years earlier, I was fortunate to meet a Swedish lady who had been part of a team of experts examining the area. She advised me to avoid Episkopi at all costs. At the time, an Englishman was trying to off load a derelict house with a large plot of almond and olive trees for twenty thousand pounds. Thankfully, it still appeared unsold as I passed by.

I was walking the steep narrow streets looking for someone to talk to, when up ahead a man stepped unsteadily from his truck. From a distance he appeared to have some form of disability, but when I enquired after the *mukhtar* he indicated that I should get into the truck. It was only when he had four hysterical attempts to find first gear that I was alerted to his whisky-laden breath filling the cab with fumes. A cigarette hung from the corner of his mouth, and I was praying that he wouldn't strike a match to light it!

Chickens were flying in all directions and goats scrambled up the rocks to avoid us. My seat belt was unusable, tangled in a mass of debris as the truck, seemingly out of control, weaved crazily down the hill. I clung to the door in case it fell off, and my head banged the roof of the cab at every pothole.

There was no sign of the *mukhtar*... and being concussed from my hair-raising descent, I felt as inebriated as the driver. I managed to convince him that I had to go in the opposite direction to him... and no! I didn't want a lift back. He pointed a crooked finger towards Kallepia, revved the engine until I thought it would hurtle through the bonnet, then disappeared - gearbox screaming - in a cloud of dust.

A track soon dipped me into the Ezousas river, and I found myself wading knee-deep through its clear waters. I followed the river northwards, slurping along the edge of a field where pink lamium and tall verbascom shone with yellow intensity against the greenery of wild fig trees. I sheltered from the sun under a dense plane tree, whose branches formed a cool archway over the river. The water was much deeper here. It swirled in small eddy's around strewn boulders and the remnants of a bridge, long since eroded by winter rains. In perfect harmony to the rippling waters, distant bird song filtered through the leaves, bringing a trance-like quality to the valley. I breathed deeply, cherishing the peace and calm before reluctantly moving out again into the sun.

My route became tougher; almost identical to the Diarizos valley. Again, I was forced to wade across the river several times until I reached a clearing. I consulted the maps. In front of me should have been a forked path... in reality, there were five different routes. I eliminated the two on my right as they appeared to circle back to the river and, keeping faith in my compass, chose the middle of the remaining three paths. I was now bearing north-west.

This was open country, my track often disappearing in the long scorched grass. My eyes were fixed on a hillside marker, and not wanting to divert from it meant forsaking shade and refreshment in a distant orange grove. With my throat parched by the heat I stopped to drink; it was then that I saw the eagles, hanging motionless like two dark shadows covering the sun.

The Bonelli's eagle is a resident of Cyprus, but its habitat is found in Kyrenia and the Troodos mountains where they nest in the cliffs or large trees. Perhaps it was their search for food that had brought them to the valley. I felt it was a rarity seeing them this close. With a wingspan of almost one and three quarter metres, their markings were unmistakable: a thick black band under their wings and long tail, made clearly visible by off-white underparts. I watched them, hoping they might dive for a morsel to eat, but as I trudged on they barely moved at all, content just to ride the hot trails of rising air.

It was noon before I reached the limestone hills. My track receded where the powdery rocks closed in, and at times it became no more than a ledge over a deep ravine. Some of these dried-up gullies are flushed with rainwater in winter: small tributaries that nourish the land and feed the main rivers. By springtime, however, they have trickled away to dust.

Since my hospital visit I had not taken my injuries lightly. I was using the painkillers as prescribed, and frequently rubbed ointment into my shin. In addition, if my knee caused problems - as it did climbing the far side of the ravine - I would reduce my ratio of paces between rests. At its peak, the track circled away from the wild barren cliffs and threaded through the vineyards and almond trees of Kallepia. It ended abruptly at a 'T'-junction. I dropped my pack to the ground and sat against a stone wall draining my flask.

There was no sign of a house... nothing, except the flight of a swallow. I watched the bird closely, its tiny form defying gravity as it skimmed the rutted track at incredible speed. Then as it neared me, it flipped a somersault and hurtled back whence it came. At different intervals other swallows dipped and dived, all returning in the same direction... to their nesting place in the village, or so I hoped. If I was wrong, the path would most certainly lead me deep into the vineyards. But after walking a hundred metres or so, some grey stone houses appeared through the trees.

Kallepia was a village of gold teeth. The first three men I

spoke with all had fifteen carat smiles. Yiannis, at the tiny supermarket, however, appeared to have left his at home. This was to be the first and only time I saw anyone chewing crisps with their gums!

Yiannis was a neat little man, his age difficult to assess. There were very few lines on his face and neck, yet his close-cropped hair was grey and his hands callused and scarred from years of hard labour. He wore a black pin-striped jacket, slightly long in the sleeves, with a matching waistcoat that sported a heavy-looking gold watch and chain. Beneath this, I could have sworn he was still wearing his pyjamas. It was a real pleasure to meet him. I played shopkeeper while he disappeared to get refreshments.

'You wait, please, for people in shop. *Endaxi*?'

I nodded, smiling to myself as he toddled away in his slippers.

Two elderly ladies arrived after Yiannis had left; neither paid for their oddments, writing in a little red book on the counter, instead. Yiannis soon returned, carrying a tray of fruit and nuts, with two large bottles of beer. He then proceeded to open boxes of crisps, handing me a handful of bags to choose from. I pointed to his book, showing him that two women had called and were asking after him. His eyes lit up, 'Ah! Maria? No problem. They wait for pension... All people wait. See?' He held the book, wetting a finger and turning the pages to show me endless lists of names and money owed.

When times were hard in Britain the 'slate' was widely used in corner shops. Now you see a sarcastic sign, like:

'Don't ask for credit - then you won't be offended'. I looked around Yiannis' shop, and in memory I was transported back fifty years in time.

His wooden counter was chipped and marked with cigarette burns. There was no till, just a drawer where Yiannis kept his takings. His little red book was kept under a sweet jar, and above his head hung a fly paper... plastered with its victims. Beside him, last year's calendar was pinned to a shelf alongside a picture of the Virgin Mary; next to which, stood assorted candles and fabric conditioners.

Around the walls, wooden shelving sagged under the weight of every product imaginable, with pigeon-holed sections for smaller items from rusty nails to laxative pills. Small labels had been stuck on the shelf fronts, marked and re-marked so many times that all prices had become a lottery. Whether stock was past its sell-by date or not, however, no-one really cared. Yiannis provided a service for the villagers... that's all that mattered to them.

He crunched away with his gums on a second bag of crisps, humming a tune as he did so - then stopping to clink glasses with mine at every mouthful of beer. The sliced apple and toffee-coated nuts tasted delicious. Yiannis seemed glad of my company - so I stayed much longer than I should have. Why not? I thought. I may never see likes of him again.

It was much cooler when I left Kallepia. A breeze wafted through the hills, complementing a pleasant downhill route that reached a tarmac road west of the village. It was a good surface for walking, and although sometimes busy with local traffic and tourist cars, today was exceptionally quiet. From here to Letimbou - the village where I planned to sleep - was only five or six kilometres away. I was hoping to meet my friends from the charity there. Maybe if I put my best foot forward, whichever that was, I would make it before they did.

This downward slope to Letimbou opened the vine-covered hills into a panorama of one hundred and eighty degrees. A jigsaw of fields, beyond which, distant mountains appeared to tremble in the simmering heat. It was the easiest end-of-day march I had experienced, arriving at the village by four-thirty - ample time to help the charity search out my bed for the night.

I sat in the coffee-shop drinking 7-up and exchanging polite conversation with its occupants, who became increasingly interested in the contents of my backpack. Their inquisition was not ill-mannered, merely an interest into anything unfamiliar. One enquired of my purpose of walking when he always used his car; another wanted to buy my sleeping bag for his father. 'When it very hot, his bed... er, how do you say?.. we'

'Move it under the stars?' I suggested... Being aware that sleeping outside was quite a common practice in the summer months.

'Ne! Ne!' he cried, fingering the soft material of the bag. 'Very nice. How much, please?'

I sympathized, but assured him I couldn't sleep without it. He was not impressed. Two minutes later, however, another drink was brought over to me, paid for by Andreas. I raised my glass to him and he winked broadly - there were no hard feelings at all.

It was five-thirty when the *mukhtar* arrived in the village, and together with Dorathy, Bett and Jim, I sat in his office sipping orange while we discussed a place of accommodation. The *mukhtar* made some unsuccessful telephone calls, intimating that now was not a good time to contact people. 'Maybe after one... two hours we find something,' he smiled.

He was a tall, slender figure, well dressed in a dark tailored suit, white-collared shirt and matching tie. His office was not as tidy - but this was not unusual. In general, Cypriots are not as precise or fanatical about paperwork as the English, but they are very shrewd in business. He suggested we stroll around the village, and led the way to a small taverna. Here we were introduced to Jeff and Rosie Adams, who sat with two friends enjoying an early evening meal out in the street.

They not only offered me accommodation but insisted on calling for another plate. I pulled up a chair, and with local trucks whizzing at my back, ate meat meze with red wine, followed by an assortment of fruit. I had hoped to see inside the Byzantine church, Agios Kyriakos, but with the sparkling wine and conversation, darkness crept in and my eyes became heavy with tiredness.

Their house was a short distance away, deceivingly small from the front gate, but once inside its rooms rambled on with tasteful furnishings and enviable space. I was taken to my room which held a most comfortable four-poster bed, and following a hot shower I returned to find Rosie feeding my dusty clothes into her washing machine. A dressing gown had been left for me, and an ice-cold beer was waiting in the lounge.

This was the other face to the coin. A remarkable difference to the condescension I had previously experienced in Armou. Jeff and Rosie were the best of British. Not just because of their generosity in taking me as a guest into their home; nor because of feeding me, as I had enough money to pay my own way. No... this was about caring; not for me as an individual, but showing a genuine interest in my efforts to alleviate the misfortunes of others: namely, the problems of mothers and their unborn babies in the hospital.

I studied my notes before sleeping... Letimbou was a medieval village, and the church I had missed earlier held a number of scenes depicting the appearances of Jesus after his resurrection. One in particular, is extremely rare: a portrayal of Christ against silvery-white radiation's in the form of an eight-pointed star.

Part of my journey for the following day was by compass. From Choulou, some eight kilometres north-east, there was nothing on my map indicating a route to Agios Dimitrianos in the north. I would have to descend into the Ezousas valley and follow its river before navigating my way out again.

Jeff woke me from a deep sleep at six-thirty. My shirt and trousers had been neatly pressed, and a breakfast of boiled eggs and cups of tea beckoned at the kitchen table. He reminded me of John Orr, the man with the pet octopus. Not by his features, but in the interesting aspects of his conversation. Even at this early hour Jeff was in top form, telling me about his family business.

The company, even though small in terms of its family-based staffing levels, was very much an international concern. It had branch offices in Cyprus, South Africa, Malaysia and Saudi Arabia, as well as their base at Kent in England. The company's business primarily covered the precision marking of athletic tracks and sports halls, including track repairs, their refurbishment and upgrading. Like most modest men, Jeff only spoke of his achievements when I prompted him. But even so, it was nice to be walking along that morning with the man who had surveyed and marked out the athletic's arena for the Olympic Games at Barcelona.

He and Rosie enjoyed walking, often along this very road to Lemona, my first village of the day. Jeff was kitted out in shorts and a matching pale blue shirt, long woollen socks and sturdy boots. He carried a long staff similar to the men I had seen on the outskirts of Episkopi: forked at one end to pin down the heads of unwelcome snakes.

South of the road to Lemona lay the deserted houses of Pitargou, and further on towards the river, we passed the stone skeletons of Kourtaka. Jeff shortly steered a path through some vineyards, and we arrived in Lemona to see a fat lady in droopy stockings opening the coffee-shop... Apart from this unexpected sight, the village had a beautiful setting. Surrounded by hectares of almond, olive and fig trees, its borders linked the great flowing vineyards that rambled southwards along the Ezousas valley almost to the sea.

Near the village church, we came upon a building which had been converted to a small brewery - a product of which, was a rather flat-tasting bottled bitter, named 'Aphrotisa'. I was enjoying Jeff's company and witty conversation, but all too soon he was shaking my hand and returning home again. We had reached Choulou by then, and he left me chatting to the locals in the modernized area of a taverna. It was situated opposite a mosque in the old Turkish quarter of the village.

Choulou had once been a mixture of Greek and Turkish families; its houses, mainly empty and drab, lined numerous dusty streets. A place one would hardly associate with King Peter 1, one of the eighteen Lusignan rulers of Cyprus. Known as the last of the true Crusaders, his character in the face of adversity was legendary, and in his conquests for the glory of religion, Pope Uban V called him 'an athlete of Christ'. The king's prowess, however, was evident in other circles. Besides his wife, Eleanor of Aragon, he also had two mistresses. His first, Joanna l'Aleman, was born c1350, somewhere in this village.

The pathway down to the river was disused and overgrown with brambles and maquis. Progress was slow, but with the sun tucked away behind gathering clouds, I edged my way between the rutted surface without relative discomfort. My plan was to pass a water mill in the valley, then continue through a copse of olive trees to a point north of a fork in the river. It didn't work. I met the river further south, forced there by a path hell bent in erratic directions. I paddled over a narrow tributary and followed my compass due north, climbing almost six hundred metres. This would be my last real test of endurance across the region's three major valleys and peaks. It was an encouraging thought.

CHAPTER 9

ON THE GRAPEVINE

It was a slow, gruelling climb. The tracks often deep ruts filled with loose slate and stones, making footholds as slippery as ice. I could see nothing ahead, but my choice of pathways proved successful, and soon after spotting the village water tower my feet met the tarmac road leading to Agios Dimitrianos. In the vicinity of its church were a number of ancient tombs, plundered long ago by robbers and archaeologists. The village itself was small, set along a narrow road that curved between its houses back to the main highway. No-one appeared; nothing roused itself except a tired cat yawning under a pomegranate tree.

On the far side of the village I headed north-east, once more enjoying the luxury of an easy descent to my overnight stop. It was early afternoon before the sun broke through, and by then I could see Kannaviou down in the valley. It was Sunday, the last day of April, and one of rest for my charity friends. I had admired their efforts for long enough; it was time to do some door-knocking of my own.

There were plenty of modern houses in the village, a forestry station and a few good-sized restaurants further along the main road. My first priority, however, was locating the *mukhtar* who would hopefully find me a bed for the night. This I did, and thirty minutes later I was basking in the shower of a nice apartment. My right shin had almost healed - the swelling was down and only the occasional twinge acted as a reminder . Yet my knee constantly needed attention; it remained a concern, throughout.

Kannaviou is near the fringes of Paphos forest, and as I sat in a restaurant waiting for mousaka and wine, the sensuous smell of pine drifted by. I was alone under a spread of eucalyptus trees watching nature's artistry at work: a setting sun was painting the western skies, reflecting its colours across the landscape, and even the sound of croaking frogs in a pool across the meadow, harmonized with singing birds.

As on most days, I left my room early. A Greek flag hung motionless at the church, and much the same as yesterday, the clouds held back a watery sun. Moving nearer the great forests, their sight and smell lent a vibrancy to the morning light. My breath exuded in white streams as I began to huff and puff, my heart pounding in response to the rising terrain. I had turned westwards now, taking a northern plane towards my first village.

The giant heads of artichokes spilled over garden walls, and a man leading his donkey to the fields waved a cheery good morning. This was Kritou Marottou, a nice village filled with greenery and splendid views that dipped through a fertile valley to the mountains beyond. The swallows had begun another busy day, and noisy sparrows chatted in the treetops as I rested outside the coffee-shop. It was a new building; traditional hard-backed chairs replaced with coloured bucket-type seats. It was oranges for breakfast, rescued earlier from a small orchard.

Except when desperation arose and I'd eaten lemons, I had become cheerfully selective. Larger, thick-peeled oranges always seemed dry and tasteless - my favourites were smaller, having a thin peel and every segment oozing with juice and flavour. The two I devoured that morning while studying my maps were scrumptious.

Near the church of Agia Marina was a narrow track which climbed a further two hundred metres to Fyti. My walk to the village was through a perfume of pine and hedgerows of wild honeysuckle. A stillness touched the roadside fields. Most of their flowers still lay in sleeping buds, awaiting a call from the morning sun. It never came; the clouds were determined to thicken.

This was a Greek village, one of a cluster of ten Greek settlements within a few kilometres of each other. It appeared empty as I approached. Old houses were locked and barred: empty shells where the cycle of life had been left to breeding swallows. Unpainted shutters hung on broken hinges, warped into strange shapes by the sun and rain. But suddenly, I was standing in the square as if in another world, surrounded by a modernized complex of houses, tavernas and coffee-shops.

'Hello, there! Good morning!'

I looked around to find a beautiful young woman smiling at me from the doorway of a nearby taverna.

'Are you Petros... The one I hear all about on the radio? The man who walks all over Paphos?' Her spoken English was better than mine!

'Good morning! Yes... I'm the crazy one.'

She laughed. 'Please come inside. We have made a collection for you.'

Her hair was long and black as ebony, its lustre matched only by the ringlets of a small girl who stood clinging to her dress. Maria gave me fifty pounds in an envelope, then offered cakes and a jug of iced lemon juice.

She had classic looks: dark sensuous eyes, high cheekbones and features like fine porcelain. Even in the simplest of movements her beauty was magnetic. Yet it's often been said that these sun-baked lands tarnish the sparkle of womanhood. The slender figure soon takes on a full maternal presence, and their features age prematurely in the sun. But feminine lifestyles have changed dramatically over the past twenty years; it was yesterday's woman who could work the land with a stamina equal to her man. Modern-day Cyprus is different. A young woman is more conscious of her diet and sustaining health and beauty. Today, I thought, that Roman sculptor would have no problem in finding his model for Aphrodite... She was here in Fyti.

At the edge of the village beside a field of poppies was a small cemetery. I paused at the gates to find the site looked clear across to the distant ocean. Those who lay

A welcome to Stroumbi

ΠΑΦΟΣ

there in peace, had found the most beautiful place to rest.

My road fell gently westwards between the orchards, and two kilometres later I was met by the swallows of Lasa. It was almost eleven o'clock, yet the only other movement in the village was a pair of feet poking through a bedstead in an open doorway. I stopped, hoping to take a photograph. A woman called out, and the toes wriggled in defiance. I approached with my camera... and a barking dog nearly had the backside from my trousers. I remember leaving in a hurry for Drymou.

From the lower mountain ranges to the sea, fossilized material has revealed that oak was one of the most common trees in the region. Its Greek name, pronounced 'drees', is significant to the village names of Drouseia, Drynia and Drymou. The latter, which I now approached, was a handful of stone houses whose gardens brimmed over with colourful geraniums.

I off loaded my backpack and sat on a bench beneath an enormous tree. A neatly printed sign told me in Greek and English that it was the 'Giant Pistashia of Drymou.' A footstep turned on the gravel path and I looked up to find a man walking towards me, leaning heavily on a blue-painted cane. He doffed his hat, asking in broken English if he might join me. I had begun to peel an orange, offering him half - but he refused with a polite, 'No thank you very much.' Then... 'I learn to speak English from soldiers in the war... At Crete,' he offered. 'English very good men... Germans, *Ohi*!' He spat in disgust, shaking his head with sadness. 'I lost many friends. You understand?'

'Of course,' I replied... 'I'm sorry.'

To every Paphian, particularly the older ones in remote areas, their village is always, 'The best in the whole of Paphos.' Most will stay in the village of their birth... all will be buried there. Aristos was no exception. He reminded me of Agathoklis from Galataria: his same wiry build, and an inner strength that defied his years. He wore a white long-sleeved shirt and a cream pullover with ragged cuffs, both tucked into a pair of brown trousers. His grey waistcoat hung unbuttoned, smudged in places by droppings of snuff.

I told him how much I liked the peaceful surroundings of his village. It cheered him up. '*Ela.* Come and see our cave. A very old place of worship,' he smiled. Aristos was pointing his stick at the sky. 'We must go... Soon it will rain.'

While I slipped on grassy slopes, the old man was as sure-footed as a goat. But I persevered, excited by the prospect of seeing the cavern because I had read that Drymou was once a place of worship to Apollo Hylates.

'When I was boy, we go inside... but now only this... See? It is here inside the rocks.' He pointed to a sealed entrance in the hillside. 'Finish now,' he said.

'You mean a tunnel under the road?'

'*Ne! Ne!* Kato dromos.'

Although there was nothing but an outline, it had strong possibilities. I was not educated in archaeological ways, but in these villages many of the old people remember strange and wonderful things, and even the most learned of scholars would be foolish indeed to disregard them.

The skies were darkening as I returned to the cross-roads. My route would gradually fall now, eventually taking me through the vast grape-producing areas of the region. But first came Drynia, an even smaller village than the last. Here, I was invited to drink Greek coffee and *zivania* with the coffee-shop owner and four locals playing cards. I obliged, but more to be sociable than out of choice... I wanted to remain sober! My interest, however, was drawn away from their game to a variety of portraits hanging around the room. One of the men called out who they were. 'Markos Drakos, Mouskos, Zakos... Fine men. All killed by the British!' he said, frostily.

I recognized General Grivas and Archbishop Makarios, and the man mellowed when I mentioned them. Then came the drawings of handsome Greek heroes from another era: Androutsos, Nikitaras and Kitsos Tzavellas... he knew them all. I returned to finish my coffee under his watchful gaze: a withering look that is often misinterpreted, for as I left he was the first to rise and shake my hand. He insisted on stopping the card game to walk me down the street, pointing me in the direction of Psathi.

The narrow path was steep and treacherous, but I was lucky - for a few hours later it would become impassable.

'You must hurry,' my companion had said. 'The rains will turn it into a waterfall.'

The path widened as I reached a green valley where donkeys roamed untethered in the lush grass. It was humid; no breeze or birds... and so quiet and still before the storm that one might hear the fluttering of a butterfly's wing. Up ahead, the track broke away in several directions. I put my trust in the swallows. Having grown fond of these delicate creatures, I followed their acrobatics to where the road widened again into Psathi. These collection of small settlements have a reputation for their embroidery, but unlike the renowned village of Lefkara, no-one was visible making lace in their open doorways. Psathi was closed... empty of life itself.

My day's journey had been a somewhat circular tour, bringing me back to the western flanks of the Ezousas valley, some two kilometres below Agios Dimitrianos. The clouds were ominous; streaked black with heavy rain over the mountains. I quickened my step, hoping to reach Polemi before the storm. But the forked lightening began to strike the mountains like a venomous reptile: recoiling at the thunder, then striking again into the heart of the forests. On the outskirts of the village I was caught in a downpour.

I sheltered under the gantry of a school, where the smell of roses and marigolds became enriched by the rain. I sat on the schoolhouse steps watching the huge raindrops bounce and clatter like pebbles down the street. I wondered just how much rain was needed in order to create the right balance for the region's abundant supply of grapes? I knew that Polemi was one of the six major wine villages in Paphos, and that apart from Panagia in the north-east, the boundaries of Letimbou, Tsada, Polemi, Stroumbi and Kathikas were joined, one village to the next, by a conglomeration of vineyards. But a prolonged enough drought would cause considerable deficit to the yield and quality of grapes. Much of the island's agricultural land had no irrigation, so without sufficient winter rains the long hot summers prove disastrous for the farmers.

Although the streets rippled with water, it was barely enough to dampen the crusty earth in the fields. In fifteen minutes the storm had blown into the sea. I walked the main road seeking refreshment of some kind, and at the first *cafenion* nibbled at a bizarre mixture of almonds, salted peanuts, sliced apple and a raw artichoke. The owner insisted it would give me strength... I experienced indigestion.

The area had once been renowned for its high quality topaz crystals, known as 'basso' - or 'baffo' - diamonds. Somewhere in the village was also a church of Byzantine origin; enlarged over the centuries, it was said to contain a painted panel in the Italian Renaissance style. But the richness of Polemi is in its soil. Derived from the decomposition of limestone rocks, it is most suited to the cultivation of vines. Passing through the village, however, my immediate vicinity was steeped in almond and apple orchards. But these soon merged again into a density of grapevines that flanked the roadside all the way to the Paphos/Polis highway. I was within one kilometre of my destination when a sit-up-and-beg tractor chugged by, its driver bidding me a warm welcome to Stroumbi.

The upper village had been severely damaged in the 1953 earthquake, suffering many casualties and loss of life. But the Stroumbi of today was a large bustling village. Rebuilt and expanded down the lower slopes, its functional style was without fuss or decorative buildings. The coffee-shop was full. I dropped my pack outside, hoping to find the *mukhtar* among the noise and plumes of cigarette smoke.

Charalambos had seen my arrival and greeted me in the doorway. There followed a procession of handshakes as he introduced me to some of the villagers, all clamouring to buy me a drink. I settled for a bottle of fizzy orange. Apparently, my charity friends had just left, and a room was already prepared for me at his house. The *mukhtar* assessed my bedraggled form. 'You look tired and hungry, my friend. Have you eaten today?' He roared with laughter when I told him, fruit, nuts and a raw artichoke. 'Come... We must go to my house for a meal, and we will drink wine while you tell me about England.'

Charalambos was a well educated man. His dark hair, flecked with grey, intimated the distinguished look of a company executive. He wore a black three-pieced suit, tailored in London, where he had studied for several years before returning to Cyprus. His wife was silent throughout our meal, listening intently as I answered her husband's questions about England: its political problems, the Royals and our football teams. But rather than eat, Georgia seemed content just to replenish the table with food; it was permanently full, even after waistlines had expanded and we were flushed with wine. On the subject of wine and grapevines I touched on a favourite topic of conversation with Charalambos. I told him that on my travels I had noticed many vineyards built in tiers. 'Why is it done this way?' I asked.

'Well, as you know, our normal rainfall in Cyprus is often very low, and where the land slopes severely this rainfall would soak away and be lost. In order to preserve it, the land is worked into platforms - each supported by dry stone walls. These help to prevent soil erosion, but more importantly, the walls retain moisture in the earth.'

'I see that irrigation to the fields is mostly confined to general agriculture, fruit orchards and vineyards on the lower coastal plains. Is this why grape production and quality sometimes suffers in the hills?'

After half a bottle of red wine and my second beer, I was pleasantly surprised by these questions... they almost sounded coherent. Charalambos' answers were enlightening.

'Yes it is. More than eighty-five per cent of the island's agricultural land is without irrigation. The total area under vines is something like twenty-six thousand hectares, and ninety-one per cent of this, yield wine grapes. You can imagine, then, how much the lack of rain affects us?'

I nodded, letting Charalambos continue as he refilled our beer glasses.

'The island normally produces two hundred million kilograms of grapes every year. Over seventy per cent of which, are purchased from the farmers by our four major wineries: Keo, Sodap, Loel and Etko. The remainder are utilized for raisins; a proportion is exported as table grapes; some are retained by the vine growers themselves for local consumption, or sold to small village wineries.' He paused to clatter his glass against mine in a toast, licking his lips with delight.

I offered another question. 'What about disease? Are the vines prone to suffer from... er?'

'Phylloxera?' He saved my memory. 'No... I think perhaps our cultivation of grapes is as ancient as the island's history. With a mild winter climate, Cyprus avoids the fog and frosts of European countries so the vines have never been attacked by this disease. Some of the varieties we have are not grown anywhere else in the world,' he added, proudly.

'I know of the black Mavro and white Xynisteri, and one... I was told about in Panagia... at the monastery.' I decided against pronouncing its name as by this time my voice was beginning to sound distinctly slurred. There was also a long pause before I remembered the question. 'Er... How many? I mean... What other vines...?'

Charalambos reeled off another twelve varieties, along with the areas where they are mostly planted. All of which I had forgotten by morning.

'... vineyards mostly cover the western and southern slopes of the Troodos mountains,' he was saying. 'These grapes are crushed immediately after harvesting and the juice fermented for wine. The edible varieties, or table grapes, are mainly from the plains between Paphos and Limassol.'

Whilst I appreciated the *mukhtar's* knowledge of the vines I was now desperately tired, and before he could fill my glass again I made my apologies to retire for the night. Georgia had made up one of the most comfortable beds of my journey. I remember nothing of my room... only the cool sheets, a firm mattress and the soft pillows under my head.

I slept until six o'clock, awakened by a cockerel crowing

outside my door. I heard Georgia chasing it away from the house with a broom - but it squawked and crowed even louder from the garden.

It was gloomy outside, a breeze soon blowing the cobwebs from my head as I walked the highway towards Polis. The road ploughed northwards between the vast areas of grapevines, their young green shoots now beginning to colour the landscape. In the west, quilted patterns of vine-clad hills spread from Kathikas, and down the eastern slopes lay the ruins of several churches. A watery sun climbed over the mountains... my fourteenth day had begun.

CHAPTER 10

THE GOLDEN COAST

Giolou occupied both sides of the main road: the old village - which I arrived in - and the more modern, where houses spread down into the eastern valley. I drank fresh orange juice with a young girl who had heard a news bulletin about me on Radio Paphos. She hailed a passing truck, asking me to wait while she found her uncle, the *mukhtar*. A short time later she returned with fifty pounds. My pockets were now bulging with money, having missed Dorathy and Bett the previous night.

Near a bridge over the Kambouras stream, two kilometres north of Giolou, the vineyards faded into citrus groves and a lush green blanket covered the land. In the hills to my left, an earthquake had rocked several villages three weeks before my arrival. Soon, I was to witness its devastation.

Loukrounou, a Turkish village above the road, was little more than dust - and ahead in the valley, Evretou had been swallowed by the waters of a dam; the only consolation being its name, the Evretou Dam. I turned east at a road junction, following the dried-up Kolojon stream and on towards a nest of Turkish villages: Sarama, Istinjon, Zakharia, Meladhia and Melandra - which once held two medieval chapels - and finally, the settlement of Trimithousa. Neolithic elements had been discovered here, and in 1833 it witnessed the surge of a revolt started by a local resident, Giaur Imam, whose followers took control of Paphos for several months. But there was nothing to be seen now except stone shells and beautiful scenery; its inhabitants joining the exodus north over two decades ago.

The way to Simou was through billowing clouds of limestone. Bulldozers were ploughing a new road, making it an unpleasant trek up to the village. Once clear of the dust, I could see the Evretou Dam down in the valley; its waters gently lapping at the windows of half submerged houses. Dark clouds threatened, casting long shadows over the dam. Yet the wind, fresh on my face, lent no ripples to the sheltered water, whose black, glossy surface lay curved and still like a dead serpent.

From Stroumbi it had taken five hours to reach Simou. I rested there until noon, checking my maps for a track down to the Stavrou tis Psokas river. Simou was as quiet as the dam. I sat on the doorstep of an empty house with my thoughts. Charalambos had been a fine host - I was only sorry to be overcome with tiredness - I'm sure his repertoire would have extended to the historical aspects of Cyprus wine as well. He would have told me of their renown in the ancient world throughout the Greek and Roman eras. How the fame of Cyprus' Commandaria - the oldest named wine in the world - began to spread far and wide. That Richard 1, King of England, celebrated with this wine, his marriage to Berengaria, daughter of the King of Navarre. And in England, thereafter,

Commandaria became the favourite sweet wine of the Plantagenet kings. My friend would have mentioned how it was featured in a great banquet known as the 'Feast of the Five Kings', given in London in 1362 in honour of King Peter 1 of Cyprus...

I took an orange from my pack, wondering if King Peter had taken his wife with him... or even his mistress, Joanna L'Aleman, from the village of Choulou?

My chosen path into the valley was, it appeared, untrodden since Roman times. In places, I was chest high in tangled vegetation, and making headway became a series of diversions. I was soaked in sweat when I reached the river, resting for a while at the Skarphos Bridge. A medieval structure that, according to my map's 'Miscellaneous Cultural' section, was now government property. As I sat there scribbling notes, the sun broke through with uncanny timing... my next village being five hundred metres above.

Exhausted by this climb, I sat at the roadside pouring water over my head. Heat was rising from the valley, turning mountains into featureless shadows and the landscape to white, powdery sand. Gone were the arbutus and pistachia trees, the golden oak and majestic pines. So indistinct was my vision that I could have been in a desert; the land I had left behind merely an illusion. Filousa, too, seemed a ghostly place. Once the site of Stone Age settlers, its houses stood in silent disarray. I found a standpipe to drink from, and dousing myself in water, recollected that many years ago the predominant motives of local crime were water and women... in that order. It was said that a Cypriot would kill someone more readily for interfering with his water supply than his wife!

A nearby door banged like a gunshot... and I almost jumped out of my boots.

I was now within five kilometres of my appointed night-spot. An easy route, that curled northwards through the ruins of Meladhia into the fig growing district that surrounded Lyso. This was a large village, and on the map boasted three churches, a school, hospital and the familiar cemetery. There were also numerous rock-cut tombs in its vicinity. I was too tired to search, though, arriving in the late afternoon hungry enough to eat a pocketful of raw beans offered by a man tending his goats. Later, after enjoying an evening meal, I tried my luck at one of the village churches.

Panagia Chryseleousa is reputed to be of Latin origin, preserving some Gothic capitals and arcading. On its doorways were faded coats of arms, but both me and my camera were forbidden inside by the heavily bolted doors. I drifted back to the coffee-shops, and on an open balcony shared a couple of beers with a retired forestry worker. His name escapes me still.

I recall his deep-set eyes and rugged, sunburned features; the calculated way he licked his bushy moustache after every mouthful of beer... 'Much too good to waste,' he had said. I also remember his carved walking stick, and the way he jabbed at the night sky in his reference to the stars. He pointed west to the faint lights curving around Chrysochou Bay, and told me a story about Aphrodite and the apple...

'As the horizon cuts the sun into a crimson half-apple, then dies in the western waves... Hesperus appears. This star is sacred to the love goddess, Aphrodite, and the apple a gift by which her priestess lured the King to his death with love songs.'

I felt his eyes searching mine for belief. I nodded, urging him to continue. But he leaned back on his stick, looking for the coffee-shop owner. 'Hey, Christo!... *Milo! Milo*!'

An apple came sailing over and he caught it, grinning as he opened the blade of his knife. 'Hesperus is Aphrodite's star,' he resumed. 'Look, Petros... You must watch! I cut the apple this way.' The old forester sliced it transversely. 'Now... Her five-pointed star will appear in each half... See?'

Sure enough the star shapes appeared, and I asked for his legend again so that I might write his words in my notebook. He was highly delighted.

When I retired to my room in the village, I found that I had covered roughly twenty-six kilometres to Lyso. Checking my route for the following day, however, revealed it would be closer to forty. I slept well... and needed to for such a long haul.

I headed west the next morning, my shadow a ten metre giant striding down towards Peristerona. The skies were cloudless again and the fields glistened with dew. Scattered vineyards appeared, but the land grew dense with the greenery of fig trees and carob: the bean of which, has a variety of uses... and Cyprus is said to produce the best quality pod in the world. Peristerona was surrounded by them.

It was a pleasant village, where two workmen stood outside its church debating the demolition of an adjacent house. I sat on a doorstep, watching in amusement. Each had selected a pick from a pile of tools, but neither it seemed, wanted to strike the first blow. Fifteen minutes later I passed them by... one rolled up his sleeves, the other stood scratching his unshaven chin. I wished them good morning.

'*Kalimera*, English! Where you go?' The muscular one mimicked my gait. 'Why walk in this heat?' he enquired.

'I have to reach Pomos tonight.'

'Bah! That's two days from here,' growled the man with whiskers. 'We have truck...'

'No thanks. I can see you're very busy,' I jested.

'Ne! Ne!' said muscles, spitting on his hands. 'We have much work. See... This house is falling down.' He slung the pick onto his shoulder ready for action. The corrugated roof of the building had caved in and a wall leaned precariously into the street.

'*Ne*, it looks dangerous,' I sympathized. 'But where do you start?'

Whiskers removed his cap and scratched his balding head this time; their debate started all over again. I moved on, listening for the industrious sound of men at work... but there was nothing except their heated voices echoing after me down the narrow street.

My route curved into a long horseshoe north of Evretou Dam, opening extensive views that swept away beneath my feet to the coast. I saw the arc of Chrysochou Bay, and beyond, the sky had fallen into the sea, making it sparkle like a million sapphires.

Along this road I came across a Christian shrine. Two small pillars stood one on top of the other, with shards of pottery concreted to its base. Inserted into the stone was an icon of a saint; opposite, stood a carob tree with several strips of rag and handkerchiefs tied to its branches. This signified an ancient custom that relates to prayer for a cure to certain disabilities or illnesses. I had read that no island of comparable size to Cyprus, holds so many ruined religious sites and buildings. The same must be said for its saints. Each one, it seems, blessed with some divine power of healing.

The village of Steni was divided by a ravine. Some of its older houses clung like eagles' nests on a rocky ledge, others had crumbled into the depths below. Across the gorge, skeletons of new buildings were under construction, and from established gardens crimson and purple bougainvillea petals splashed over the roadway. It was too hot to side-track my journey, but somewhere in the vicinity lay the ruins of a monastery. Its church had been heavily buttressed following an earthquake in the sixteenth century, but Chrysolakourna is remembered for a more sinister cause: Turks had seized and executed the monastery's last abbot, hanging him in 1821.

Walking away from Steni, I began looking for breakfast. Fig trees were now fully clothed in green, brushing the ground with their heavy branches, but the fruit was small and not really edible. Further on, searching a copse of orange and lemon trees, I came across a man sitting at a table in the shade. He wore a cloth cap, with brown trousers and braces over his pyjamas. I smiled to myself;

Old church at Limni mines

nothing surprised me anymore.

'*Kalimera sas,*' I said, cheerfully.

He nodded his head. 'I know you coming, my friend... English, eh?.. but you sing Irish song.'

'Sing? Oh, that was way back!' I said in surprise.

'*Ne*... But I hear very good. *Ela*... Sit with me.' The old man fumbled for another chair. His pale blue eyes shone, and he smiled with pleasure when I shook his outstretched hand... it was only then that I noticed he was blind.

'You must be hungry. Wait... I have food,' he said, wandering back along a path to a small gate. He called his wife, and soon afterwards I was eating fresh crusty bread and fruit.

Christos was a nice man, and like many of his age group, had fought alongside the British army in the Greek islands. Like the man in Drymou, he had also learned his English from the soldiers and nurses who looked after him when he lost his sight. But even after all this time, he told me, the land had never changed.

'I noticed some new houses being built on the far side of the ravine...'

Christos held up his hand. 'No, Petros... Here, my friend. All around us. My land!' he cried. 'Every tree, flower and every bird... I still see them.' His hand touched his temple. 'Pictures,' he smiled... 'I keep all of them here.'

I listened intently for the sounds he could hear through the trees... I heard nothing but rustling leaves. He could smell thyme and almonds in the fields... and yes, somewhere a lark was singing. Christos had been blind since the age of twenty-three, yet these vivid pictures and sounds coloured his words in a poetic imagery that would have moved the hardest of men. I sat with him for half an hour... finding words difficult when the time came to say good-bye.

Down gentle slopes the small hamlets and ruined churches began to fade away. Agios Isidoros, the last of this huddle of villages was now behind me. These western hills are honeycombed with mines, and legend says that from here to the sea the roads were once paved with copper. A rich vein that run from Skouriotissa, north of the Green Line down to Polis. The Romans mined a seam so thick and pure that even thirty years ago, excavating as they did then with modern equipment, it proved difficult to match Roman skills.

At Pelathousa, an old couple who gave me fruit and water, told me their parents remembered that copper-workings from Roman times was a common sight in the hills. So, too, were the scattered tombs that contained the remains of early miners. The island's copper mines are among the oldest in the world. And it was the Romans who developed the industry, sinking mine shafts to inconceivable depths to extract the highest grade ore. They called it 'aes Cyprium', and in the medieval forms of chemistry, copper was said to relate to the sign of Aphrodite.

I could clearly see the 'Golden Bay', from Pelathousa, sweeping through the town of Polis and onward to the wild beauty of Akamas. The vast ocean lay still... now violet in colour, broken only by a peninsula and the pocket harbour of Latsi. I crossed over dried up streams and a dusty road that ran to Mavroli, reaching an area where the land assumed a bleak, synthetic face. It was a desolate site known as Limni Mines.

A century before, the limestone dust covering my boots was a huge lake, and beneath it - a labyrinth of Roman shafts, tunnels, ladder ways and drainage systems, plummeted to depths that defied human endurance. Galen, a Roman physician, described the air at the bottom of a mine as suffocating, and smelling of chalcitis and iron rust. He spoke of the naked slaves that carried jars in great haste so as not to remain long under the ground. How many suffocated; what numbers died, entombed as the earth and rock caved in around them, is futile to guess. Standing there was a strange experience. I was struck by the irony of own presence: at sightseeing in a place where so many had perished. It was a graveyard without inscription or flowers... only generations of dust.

I followed my footprints back to the path, sheltering in the shade of a ruined church - where tapers lay unused, and icons stood in shallow recesses waiting for reverence. Even inside the coolness of its walls I perspired freely. Like me, my boots were also showing signs of wear, their thick carbonized soles scuffed and battered by the rough mountain tracks. My biggest problem now, however, was dehydration. Walking throughout the searing heat of daylight hours had taken its toll. Despite some excellent meals since day one, I had already sweat and burned away six kilograms of body weight.

From the church, I compassed a route through scrub and

scattered trees to a roadway, beyond which, lay the remains of Magounda. Drained by the long trek, I had to force my weary bones across the Magoundas riverbed and the two remaining kilometres to Argaka. Here, sleeping under a shaded terrace of vines, I found Savvas, the *mukhtar*.

He was a jovial character, with an infectious laugh that was in full flow watching me drink half a jug of lemon juice. 'What a crazy man!' His eyes twinkled, and I knew what was coming next... 'No-one walks in Cyprus,' he chuckled. Then, more seriously. 'Tell me... How far have you come?'

'From Petra tou Romiou,' I replied.

His eyes popped and his mouth fell open. 'No?.. Panagia!' he cried, filling up my glass until it brimmed over. He shook his head in disbelief. 'All in a day... Here. Please drink.'

It was my turn to laugh. I explained my route and Savvas nodded, approvingly. He looked embarrassed. 'Forgive me. You are a fine man. What you do for the hospital is very nice. But you must rest. My wife will bring you food, then we go to my village square. *Endaxi*?'

I thanked him, and minutes later tucked into salad, thick slices of ham, olives and lashings of yoghurt. His wife moved gracefully to and fro, ensuring that I had sufficient to eat and drink. Her smile growing wider as I cleared my plate. Meanwhile, Savvas had gone inside the house. I heard him on the telephone - then returning in a flourish, he said we should go. He had already given me a hundred pounds, but not satisfied with this he proceeded to drive me out to a large warehouse.

It was a depot used for weighing and storing citrus fruits and vegetables from the local farmers. There, he cajoled his friends - shouting my cause - and a further eighty pounds went into my pocket. With the adrenalin flowing now, he zoomed us away on screaming tyres up the hill to the village. He stopped several trucks on the way, and money was passed over the street through cab windows. Savvas finally invaded the coffee-shop before we said our good-byes at his house. His face was a picture when I told him that his efforts had raised the greatest single donation to date. I had counted out two hundred and ten pounds.

Although it was a sideways move, I grew tired of the tracks and headed for the sea. With a better surface underfoot I knew I could make up any lost time.

As in all of Paphos, the land rises from the sea to the mountains. Lying at the foot of these western hills is a fertile land rich in banana plantations and citrus groves that stretch for eight kilometres along the coast. It must be difficult now to find any village without agricultural means. But until the turn of the century they relied solely on animals and their own stamina to work the land. The most significant improvement was the change from dry farming: cereal cultivation and the keeping of livestock, to farming with fruit and vegetables as their main crops. In addition, water companies were formed and the government built roads, which made the marketing of produce much easier.

Combined with the availability of water during hot summer months, this gave the villagers new incentives, and by the 1940's tractors began to benefit their output. Potatoes and carrots, along with the planting of citrus trees complimented the widespread growth of vineyards, and ten years later they became a feature on everyone's land. By 1968 it was rare to find any farmer without some land under trees. In the past, most villagers were peasant farmers, but with irrigation systems operational, a good income from vegetables and citrus fruit was realized. The region's agricultural land has now become both profitable and highly valued.

I approached the heart of this alluvial plain in the form of Gialia: a village reputed for its quantity of melons and a late crop of oranges - said to be the best on the island. Other main harvests seemed to be lemons, grapefruit, bananas, avocados, tangerines and grapes - but a wide variety of fruit is also cultivated in the region, namely: apples, apricots, cherries, figs, peaches, pears, plums and pomegranates.

Houses struggled up the valley to the ruins of a rare circular church, known as Agios Kornutos. The traveller, Enlart, wrote that he recognized it to be a church of trefoil plan from the Byzantine period. A Stone Age site, and two more Byzantine churches were discovered higher in the forest hills, but time was not waiting for me - my route veered back to Kato Gialia.

Twenty years earlier, its surrounding area had been largely re-planted with trees following a disastrous forest fire. But now, to travel due east from here to Livadi, is to discover one of the island's most attractive and isolated locations. The dense forests there and in the Cedar Valley beyond, are much more extensive than earlier this century. The late Winston Churchill can be accredited for improving this depleted forestry after 1907, by allocating funds to Cyprus for an immense tree planting project.

North of Nea Dimmata, I watched the sun sink into the ocean. Lazy white-capped waves caressed the shore in distant coves, and a premature darkness closed in as the forests of Tilliria touched the roadside. The only chinks of light through this dense woodland came from the gorges and narrow streams. It was approaching dusk when I reached Pomos.

The charity had arranged accommodation for me in the village, but I mistakenly passed a coffee-shop where my host sat waiting. A friendly couple came to my rescue, however, and invited me into their home. It was a modern house, with marble floors and tasteful furnishings, but with three young boys there was no spare room. Nevertheless, they gave me nourishment and made telephone calls to secure a place for me to stay. By ten o'clock I was tucked up in bed fast asleep.

Pomos was my most northern village in the region. I was three kilometres away from Nicosia's boundary, and a further three from Kokkina, a tiny village guarded by Turkish troops. This is the only occupied territory distanced from the infamous Green Line that carves the island into two pieces. So named, apparently, when a British RAF officer in charge of peace-making on the island in the sixties, drew a line on a map to signify where the Greeks and Turks met at the time of violence. In drawing this line east to west he used a green pencil... Not necessarily an appropriate division... but nonetheless, an authentic story.

Yet another Stone Age site had been found near Pomos, containing two steatite idols of very fine workmanship. But arriving late - then leaving head down against the rain, I saw little of the village. On its outskirts, the shower passed over and I began to take in the beauty of my surroundings. I was retracing my steps from the previous night, passing a sculpture of sandstone rocks that bathed in the silent sea. There was no sky looking east, it was shrouded in pine trees. Deep gorges knifed through the forest, but their scars faded into mountains whose peaks disappeared into the mist. From the Akamas peninsula, the ocean curved towards me in layers of vivid greens and blues. A western breeze drifted in but the sea was like a pond, rippled by the casting of a stone.

I strode on, time and distance slowly ticking away. Paphos forest stretched as far as I could see on the eastern flanks, but in front of the trees the roadside began to level into fields of produce. I was hoping for a banana breakfast - but there was none to be had. I settled for an orange, and sat on the deserted beach watching a large number of bee eaters gliding and swooping over the orange groves.

They are one of the island's most colourful birds. Usually seen between April and October, they feed on insects - including bees and wasps. In flight they resemble a beautifully coloured swallow, with rich red-brown under parts, bright yellow throat and blue breast. I had never seen so many flying together; it was a brilliant display.

I passed by Nea Dimmata again, but no-one appeared except a man painting an upturned boat. I waved without stopping, thankful for the few clouds that shielded the sun. Past the plantations and the road to Argaka, the forests behind me dwindled to a green tufted carpet. It was mid-day before I rested again, finding shade in some old buildings near a jetty. A sign, red with rust, could barely tell me this was the 'Cyprus Sulphur and Copper Company Limited. Limni Mines.'

This company had been formed in 1919, and although resuming its predecessor's mining activities, it embarked on a scheme of open casting the area and of stacking and leaching the minerals mined. By this method, the precipitate produced an eighty per cent copper content. No-one can begin to contemplate what richness the Romans excavated, but in the Troodos foothills alone they left more than a million tonnes of slag-heaps behind them.

At Mavroli, the road began edging away from the shore. I was now in sight of Polis and more than half way around Chrysochou Bay. Through a mixture of good fortune and typical Cypriot generosity, my charity had acquired a two night stay for me at a hotel in the town. I was hungry, my clothes were caked in dust and sweat... and I relished the thought of a long, steaming hot bath.

CHAPTER 11

AKAMAS

There were more people in the municipal square that afternoon than I'd seen on my entire journey. Tourists mainly, checking out gift shops, eating meals or snacks outside a maize of restaurants and cafes, or just wandering around aimlessly with their children in tow. I ordered an ice-cold beer, nibbling at the complementary crisps that came with it. A Japanese family were in a frenzy of excitement at the next table, clicking cameras at a group of swallows that fluttered among dozens of nests clinging to building walls. Inside one of the shops below, a barber was making noises with his clippers... but little else. The head he appeared to be working on was completely bald.

I finished my beer, and entered a bank in the square to change some currency. A young cashier recognized me from the television news, and promptly rushed around her colleagues making a collection; it was a nice, and most rewarding gesture. But I was also thankful that Bett and Jim were due at the hotel to relieve my bulging pockets, for I was carrying almost five hundred pounds in donations. They were waiting, on time as usual, and my room at the hotel Marion - courtesy of Michalakis, the general manager - was ready for occupation.

It was a comfortable twin-bedded room, with en-suite bathroom facilities, a dressing table, small bedside cabinets and telephone, two easy chairs and ample wardrobe space. Behind the draped curtains a door led to a private balcony with a pleasant view. If this wasn't grand enough, the hotel receptionist rang to say that Michalakis had invited me to eat and drink whatever I required during my stay. It was a most generous offer... but one I could not abuse.

I lay in the bath up to my eyes, soaking muscles and bones that had been punished for more than four hundred kilometres. Basking in this luxury was a far cry from my first night trying to settle on a rocky slope beside the Diarizos river.

That evening I sat out on the balcony looking at distant hills yet to climb. But their silhouettes appeared much kinder than the rugged peaks I had left behind. This was the high Akamas... a place that was to reveal a mixture of beauty and sadness. When the night sky darkened, I lay on my bed listening to the driving rain sweep over the town. I slept until dawn.

Breakfast was self service. I sat alone eating boiled eggs and toast, then spent the next few hours out on the balcony checking my notes and maps for the following day. By late morning, skies became ominous and the heavens opened again. It seemed my day of rest was well timed, but little did I realise that even worse storms lay in the hills waiting for my return to duty.

I strolled around the town that night dodging showers, until a downpour finally drove me into the shelter of a makeshift taverna. Here, in someone's garage space covered by an orange tarpaulin, sat three well-to-do couples dressed in smart, casual evening wear. There is no doubt that these same people in England would never dream of eating in a substandard restaurant - let alone a garage! Thus, in their contrary ways, the English are comical to observe.

Their tables had rusty legs and the chairs seemed like rejects from a local coffee-shop. A string of light bulbs led from the house, and while several fizzed and popped in the rain, two of them survived to light the improvised eating place. There were six usable tables, the seventh held a stainless steel bowl which caught dripping rainwater from the tarpaulin. Into this scene strode the owner carrying uncovered plates of food from his kitchen, twenty metres away. He placed two plates of rain-spattered pork chops, vegetables and baked potato on a table and, smiling broadly, returned for the salad. Again, this was freshened with rainwater, but the middle-aged couple simply thanked him and tucked into their meal with gusto.

The Cypriot was an amiable fellow trying to earn a living, yet for this type of customer to accept these conditions was a mystery. Two more journeys, and two more perfectly satisfied couples later, the old man greeted me by flicking crumbs off my table with a tea towel. I settled for *kleftiko*, which simmered nicely in a clay oven beside me; it was heavily scented with bay leaves and origanum... and raindrop-free, it tasted delicious.

Rain hammered down like stair rods, and the tarpaulin

sheet creaked under the assault. It had not been sloped to cater for bad weather, merely as an impromptu gesture of a roof. My comical vision of its collapse, however, did not materialize. When the storm passed I returned to my hotel, wondering what on earth the English folk would tell neighbours back home, or their illustrious friends at the bridge club about dining out under a tarpaulin roof... Somehow, I doubt if they ever would.

Polis is a sprawling town, occupying part of a site that was originally the city-kingdom of Marion, founded by Athenians in the seventh century B.C. It survived a succession of wars until Ptolemy 1 razed it to the ground in 312 B.C. A later member of the dynasty, Ptomely Phyladelphus, rebuilt the city and named it Arsinoe in honour of his sister. This new city held its name during the Roman and Byzantine periods, but it was then changed to Polis by the Lusignans. Under their rule Polis became one of the five important bailiwicks of the district. Its whole area is surrounded by a necropolis, and over the years thousands of tombs have yielded a variety of artefacts and imported pottery. From Arsinoe came the island's finest funeral stele, a masterpiece of relief carving from the fifth century B.C.

In a vague search of some fragment of history, I ventured back next morning towards the seashore. But wading through high reeds and bamboo the ground became silted, leading only to a barren stretch of mud-flats. Nothing remained of these ancient cities, even their tombs seemed to have vanished.

My arrangement that morning was to meet Jim near the harbour of Latsi. So leaving Polis and Prodromi behind, I ambled along at an easy pace, enchanted by a scene of ever-changing colours. Rainfall had moistened the fields and the air was fresh with exotic perfumes, but a short distance from Latsi, thunder began to growl in the hills. I quickened my step. Jim had shown a great interest in joining me to cross the high Akamas. He chose the worst few hours possible.

Since my last visit, the tiny fishing port of Latsi had changed almost beyond recognition. Shopping complexes, apartment buildings, restaurants and even banks had stretched in both directions along the coast. I passed a new landscaped area with lawns, flowers and shrubs - complete with fully matured palm trees transported from Nicosia, and recently transplanted in the gardens. A far cry from the seclusion I remembered when my wife and I used to picnic on its deserted beaches.

An ancient jetty lies beneath the waves, and a sunken breakwater shelters its picturesque harbour. But now, extended restaurants spill out onto its wooden pier - competing for the increasing surge of tourists. Like other previously unspoiled areas, good business is done here... but who in their right mind, I wondered, wanted to replace natural beauty with concrete? Latsi had become synthetic.

Jim was waiting, and after a brief rest we set out into a drizzle of rain. Ahead of us, the waves scattered pebbles on the shore leaving small inlets white with foam. Against a darkening sky I saw an island: Agios Georgios, and somewhere beyond at Cape Arnaouti, the very tip of Cyprus disappeared into the sea. This was the Akamas peninsula... the priceless jewel of Paphos.

It is a place of magical charm: rich in bird life, fauna and flora - as well as being diverse in its geological formations. A profusion of wild flowers carpet the whole area in springtime, many of them rare and endemic to Cyprus... All, in a mystical way, flourishing since the days of Aphrodite. The peninsula's name is said to originate from a Greek mythological hero, Akamas, the son of Theseus, who founded 'Akamantis' when he arrived in Cyprus following the Trojan war. But legend is strongest in its belief that this was the meeting place of Aphrodite and her beloved Adonis.

It was here in the Akamas forest where Adonis, out hunting one day, paused to drink from a stream. He was startled to see Aphrodite bathing in the crystal waters of a nearby pool, and dazzled by each others beauty they fell in love. But the couple were betrayed to the gods and Aries cast a web of gold over them, saying that Aphrodite would have to marry a mortal... and Adonis be punished by death. And so it happened. Badly gored by a wild boar, his life's blood ebbed away as he lay in the arms of Aphrodite. They say the mountain rains still weep for Adonis, and rivers forever lament the sorrow of Aphrodite. And when each winter turns to spring, she will call forth the anemone so that Adonis may be born again in the beauty of a flower.

Aphrodite's love for Adonis and the young god's cruel death is renowned, and was even featured as the theme of an opera. Written in 1682 by John Blow, 'Venus and Adonis' had to wait more than two hundred years for publication. It was performed at the Aldeburgh Festival in 1956. In ancient times, too, festivals in honour of the lovers were important cultural events. Homer's 'Hymn to Aphrodite' is believed to have been written for the Adonia and Aphrodisia festivals of Paphos.

It was this charismatic blend of legend and appeal that inspired the historian, Hogart, to describe the Akamas peninsula as the most beautiful place on the island. It seems inconceivable, therefore, that such a treasure might well be plundered by a government's weakness towards developers and capital gain. Already, suburbia approaches its southern coastline, and with Latsi expanding to the very edge of its northern shore, it seems inevitable that another major part of Cyprus' heritage will be lost forever beneath yet another needless conglomeration of hotels and restaurants.

A forty million pound project had been proposed under pretence and empty promises. A study which stated, that once developed, the Akamas region should belong to the local population... It always has - so why change it? The study went on to highlight a plight of the Akamas and its dying villages, intimating the necessity to create development opportunities that would benefit both inhabitants and tourists, alike. In short, despite their assurances to protect the environment, they want a money-spinner... a concrete jungle - not the greenery of a forest.

This plan had been drawn up by consultants appointed by the World Bank, and initially rejected outright by the Paphos community. But for how long can they hold out? The biggest landowners in Cyprus are the Church, and whilst a legal restriction once meant that only half a per cent of land could be used for development, the Bishopric of Paphos has now been granted a massive fifteen per cent by the present government. As you pause at the roadside to gaze at these aesthetic hills, one wonders how long it will be before the juggernauts are released to devour its splendour.

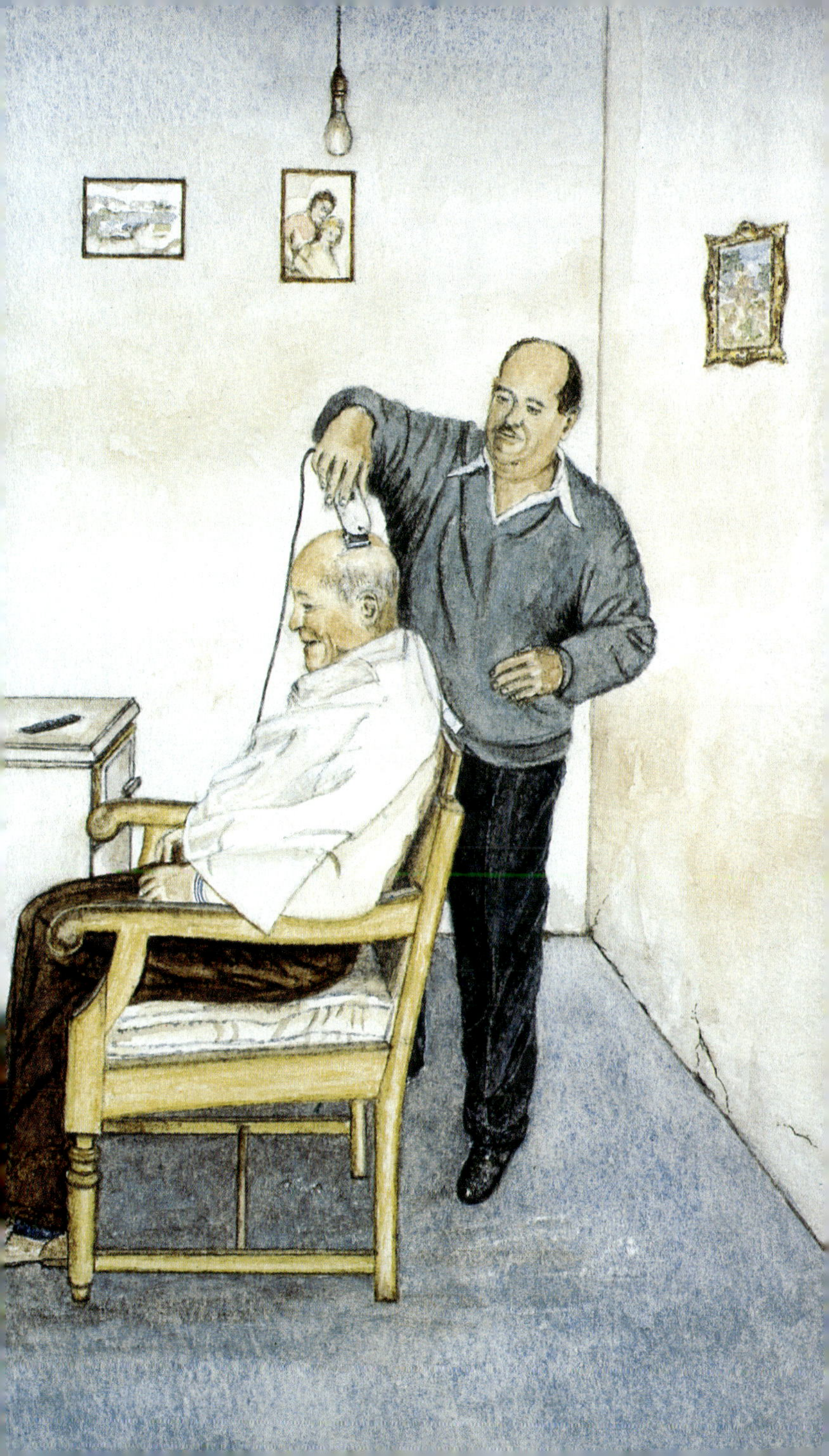

Where the road swung inland towards Neo Chorio, it began raining hard. Jim and I found shelter at a bus stop and donned our protective clothes. Me into an expensive all-in-one suit that zipped up to my chin - 'normally worn by yachtsmen' - the label indicated, and supposedly waterproof. It wasn't... but I felt good. While on the other hand, Jim sported ordinary trousers and an imaginative top he had conjured up, with head and arm holes cut out of a dustbin liner! His outfit came complete with a straw hat... which was later demolished by hailstones.

Thunder began to explode around us, but undeterred, we squelched our way up the hill towards the village. The slower we went the heavier it rained, and my suit began to leak like a colander. The road became a fast flowing stream that ran through the lace holes of our boots. And the weather gods, enraged by our defiance, unleashed bolts of lightning that scorched the hills and lashed rain into us with the force of a fireman's hose.

The island has suffered many times from drought, and it is recorded in the time of Constantine that no rain fell on Cyprus for thirty-six years. It was now making amends. We reached a village taverna looking like two stray, and drowning cats. With our so-called waterproofs left by the door, we sat huddled around a portable heater forming a pool of dripping water. Our only consolation being the tasty ham rolls and Mars bars Jim had brought along for lunch.

A few months before we were washed up in its streets, Neo Chorio had been the centre of attention. Three kilometres away, a large cavern was investigated by a Dutch expert in climbing and cave exploration. For centuries this pothole had inspired awe and superstition. In wintertime, steam could be seen rising from the hole and villagers insisted the place was haunted by evil spirits. This steam being a dragon's breath, or some other mythical beast that lurked in the depths below. But when a team of explorers descended some fifty metres on ropes, they made important discoveries.

A labyrinth of caves spread for two hundred and fifty metres through a forest of multicoloured stalactites that clung to the walls in sleek sculptured forms. Skeletons and arrow-heads were also found, lending theory to habitation or a place of refuge. Of dragons there were none... the 'breath' being confirmed as hot summer air trapped inside the cavern, seeping out during winter. Jim's shout for another beer dispersed my thoughts on dragon slaying.

I found him to be a congenial man... and great company. A ruggedly handsome Scot, who soon lifted my dampened spirits. He used to play semi-professional football in Scotland, winning cups and league titles with several clubs, and serving as player, coach and finally club manager at Broughty Athletic over a fourteen year period. Jim had also worked as a talent scout for two English teams: Rotherham United and Luton Town. He is still a qualified Scottish Football Association coach - so it could be said, without contradiction, that he knew his football.

It had stopped raining, but angry black clouds hung low and still over the hills. From the church we headed south, leaving the Akamas forests behind for a scattering of olive and carob trees. Jim's amusing soccer stories soon passed the time in reaching Androlikou, which appeared as one of the best preserved settlements I had seen.

My notes explained it as a once prosperous Turkish village, supposedly inhabited now by one family, a thousand goats, some chickens, sheep and a few pigs. The animals roamed everywhere. Most houses were still intact except for missing doors and windows, and several contained bales of straw and animal fodder. We finally saw a house with a door but no sign of humans inside, only an enormous sow sadly nudging her dead piglet. We pressed on, the land climbing steeply towards the heights of Drouseia.

Cyprus has around eighteen hundred different species of flowering plants: a rich and diversified flora which is primarily responsible for its high butterfly population. In normal conditions we would have seen many interesting varieties that morning. Yet we had reached much wilder countryside now; not in trees or vegetation, but its very emptiness imposed a feeling of immobility. You walked without progress... nothing moved closer. Trapped in this great void by a rainstorm, we seemingly trudged into the clouds. Almost total darkness descended, and visibility closed to five metres. Our boots sank into the softened limestone, tying calf and thigh muscles into knots as the mud stuck to our soles like cement.

The rain turned to sleet, and suddenly we were battered with whopping hailstones. I ground to a halt with exhaustion, watching Jim disappear ahead of me. The storm raged and I could barely hear his shout, but over the ridge he had found shelter. It was a strange, yet welcome sight. For there, as if perched on a cloud, was a solitary house with Jim hammering on its door. No-one answered, and we stood shivering together under a leaking canopy.

After a minute or so, the door creaked open just enough for an eye to peep at us. It was no surprise that it slammed shut again. Faced with Jim in a bin liner and battered straw hat - and me in a white cap and sky blue suit, the old man must have thought we were aliens from another planet. Fortunately, he did have second thoughts, and unbolted the door to invite us in.

I estimated our refuge to be on the outskirts of Fasli, a Turkish village some five kilometres north-west of Drouseia. Our host lived alone, a frail man who beckoned us to share the warmth around his small paraffin heater. With a gold-toothed smile he produced a bottle of *zivania* and a dish of peanuts from a cabinet... followed by a chunk of stale bread from his jacket pocket. Jim declined, but I was glad to let a glass of *zivania* thaw my freezing limbs.

Try as we may, we could not understand his dialect, nor he our limited Greek. Most of the time we sat smiling and nodding to each other. Jim, whose Greek vocabulary was much better than mine, tried in vain to find a suitable word for toilet. The old man just sat there shaking his head. I was desperate... and finally had to gesticulate the motions. I stood unzipping my suit, then simulated the same with my trousers. The old man roared with laughter. 'Ah!' he chuckled, pointing to the door. *'Ne. Exo! Exo!'*

I went outside. The toilet door was off its hinges, and dragging it open disturbed two chickens roosting inside, their flapping wings depositing my hat in the mud. I tried several times but the toilet wouldn't flush, its rusty chain finally snapping in my hand. It was a bad day... the only bright spot being patches of blue sky I could see through the roof.

The storm had passed, but our walk to Drouseia was through a wind that made our wet clothes cling like icy blankets. Spent hailstones piled up like snowdrifts, and temperatures plummeted along the open road. To our left lay the remains of Pittokopos, while unusual rock formations began to refine the barren landscape. This so-called breeze that sliced through us, is known by locals as 'Drouseia' meaning 'cool and fresh'. Jim and I referred to it with a few other names before we reached the village. We were in a sorry state by then, gratefully accepting the first offer of refreshment that came along.

The house contained a large family. Grandma was tending a babe in arms, while two teenage daughters and a toddler stared at our weather-beaten forms in disbelief. Their mother kindly served us Nescafe and biscuits as we sat at the foot of a double bed talking to her husband. He had dressed to go out on an early morning shoot, but sent scurrying back by the weather, had returned to bed... still in full camouflaged uniform. He sat up, arms folded likc a military general, showing great interest in our 'manoeuvres' of the day. But being so cramped for space I was having to turn round to answer his every question.

Both the coffee and their conversation warmed us, and once in the street again I noticed Jim smiling to himself.

'Did you find the guy in bed amusing?' I asked.

'Aye... He was that, alright... But how was your coffee?' Jim began to crease up with laughter.

'Coffee? Oh, fine... Gritty towards the bottom but...' I

could say no more as Jim was in hysterics, barely able to explain that each time I turned to speak with the 'general' in bed... his 'wee bairn' had been dunking his biscuits in my cup!

With narrow winding streets and friendly people, Drouseia seemed a nice village; its earliest settlers were reputed to be Arcadian. There were several coffee-shops, tavernas and even a popular hotel for those who preferred the tranquillity of Akamas to that of beach holidays. But this was not the appropriate weather for either. Thunder still rumbled in the valleys, and although my overnight stay was little more than a kilometre away, we suffered yet another soaking.

Jim and I were fortunate to find a pleasant taverna at Inia. We sat trying to dry out in front of a calor gas fire. The owner lit a second one, and the steam from us fogged out the taverna windows. My backpack was sodden, but with everything protected inside plastic bags I retrieved my warmest change of clothes: a pair of tartan pyjamas and a sweater. Seeing Jim's plight, an old-timer went home and returned with a woolly sweater for him. The big Scot thanked him... and changed his shredded bin liner. An hour - and two brandies later - I began to feel blood circulating again.

That night, I stayed a few doors away from the taverna but had little sleep. Georgios, the old-timer I stayed with, was still traumatized from the recent earthquake. He made no attempt to get into bed. I lay awake in the next room listening to him pace up and down the marble floor. I felt both sorry and helpless trying to reassure him, but he would only smile and shake his head at my offers to make coffee. His light stayed on all night. Sometimes, in the early hours, I could hear the creak of his rocking chair echoing through the house...

CHAPTER 12

EARTHQUAKE ZONE

Walking day after day across this vast region, my thoughts often wandered away from time, distance and the beauty around me. I would look without really seeing; sights and sounds were unintentionally lost to the subconscious. In these moments it is the unusual or unexpected that sharpens your focus. This was my first day without flowers. A cold wind searched the fields - but nothing stirred, their colours destroyed by the storms.

My road led to a horseshoe bend, around which, curved the north-western tip of vineyards spreading from Kathikas. On a ridge above me were two small villages: Kato and Pano Arodes, so named after the Greek island of Rhodes by their original owners the Knights Hospitallers. This was now an area almost destroyed by earthquake.

In the past, seismic activity in Cyprus has been notably less than that of Turkey and Greece. The island is said to be located on the Cyprian and Hellenistic Arcs which separate the huge African and Eurasian Plates. These plate edges are zones of strong seismic movement, and severe earthquakes are known to have shaken the island long before the days of Christ.

Two distinct epicentres are believed to exist off the Paphos coast, each estimated to lie between twenty and thirty kilometres out to sea. The first, situated midway from Petra tou Romiou to the harbour at Kato Paphos, was probably responsible for the more destructive earthquakes in the Roman and Byzantine periods. This century, however, the majority of damage has originated from an area off the Akamas coast between Koppo island and Cape Drepanum. This region has recorded several tremors since the disaster of 1953 which killed forty people, left one hundred injured and over four thousand homeless.

Six weeks had passed since February's earthquake, which had registered 5.2 on the Richter Scale and sent shock waves as far as Israel and Lebanon. I entered Kato Arodes, hoping that by now the aftermath would be well under control. It was not. Sadly, I confirmed earlier news reports of the continuous plight of villagers through government delays in providing alternative shelter and property repairs. Considering that around one hundred houses had been destroyed or badly damaged in the area, I saw only three men working on this carnage over a two day period.

Kato Arodes had not suffered badly. Some old green painted doors signified its Turkish origin, and a few holiday homes appeared occupied. I thought perhaps these could be some people from the second village, where more than twenty families had been made homeless. The upper village of Pano Arodes was one of complete devastation.

Walking its streets resembled the after effects of a bomb blast: properties had been shuffled like a pack of cards by the impact, with almost every house carrying a sticker that stated, 'Dangerous Building'. Here and there, sheltered away from buttressed houses, small tents had been erected. But they appeared of flimsy design, more suitable to summer conditions - yet amazingly, they had survived yesterday's storms. Some dwellings had corrugated sheets nailed across gaping holes, others just makeshift plastic. A number had lost their top storey's, and most cottages were just a pile of wood and stones. Only the surviving blue painted doors and shutters intimated a Greek existence; its grim and disjointed image mirrored the many decaying Turkish villages I had previously passed through.

The church of Agios Kelandion had lost its bell tower, and masonry crumbled along its roof supports. A large army tent had been erected among nearby trees, and inside, a priest conducted morning service for his people; their hushed prayers being the only sound I would hear as I walked through the village.

A government spokesman had estimated the overall earthquake damage at between two and three million pounds... and to restore Pano Arodes alone would easily incur a third of that.

My intended path through the vineyards was thick in limestone mud. I opted for an easier route, and although twice the distance, I at least stayed on dry tarmac. At the cross-roads to Drymou, a winding slope descended into a valley; its rocky hillsides carved and stepped like a Roman theatre. In the arena below stood Kritou Terra. This was one of the most attractive, and seemingly unscathed villages in the area. It nestled in an oasis of greenery, and at its entrance, traditional water springs and a pleasant taverna had been skilfully restored.

This work had been carried out as part of the Laona Project, which also restored several houses in the village in order to encourage and accommodate visitors. It was a viable alternative to the mass development of tourist complexes which would destroy an already fragile environment. The project pioneered a strategy in which local villages were offered technical and financial help in the restoration of a few selected properties, thereby attracting a sensible number of visitors to assist the village economy.

By the end of the Laona Project, restoration was completed on twenty-six buildings in five villages, including a taverna, a guest house, two Byzantine churches and a listed monument. During its operations, however, there also arose the need for environmental awareness and education. To address this requirement, a charitable foundation evolved, namely: the Cyprus Conservation Foundation. The first of its aims was to provide an Environment Studies Centre to cater for both Cypriot and foreign youngsters. It would introduce and educate schoolchildren to the island's natural and cultural environment, thus increasing their sensitivity towards its preservation.

After strolling through the village and collecting a donation from its *mukhtar*, I found myself standing outside what was once a disused schoolhouse. This forgotten corner in Kritou Terra had now been superbly restored, and the village rightly honoured with the island's first Environment Studies Centre.

I returned to the water springs, ignoring a more picturesque route that ran past the remains of an old laundry. This was no more than a series of holes in a bed of rock, where the womenfolk once did the family wash, using wood ash as a detergent. The track then crossed over fields before eventually reaching the village mosque at Terra. But wanting to keep dry, I followed a sign-posted road across the gorge. Along these sheltered verges I found a sprinkling of flowers: asphodels, pink vetch, buttercups and field marigolds, which had managed to hide their heads from the storms.

Terra is one of the oldest villages in Cyprus. Remains of a Stone Age site lie in the valley, and the village itself has been continuously inhabited since Roman times. Near the schoolhouse was a stretch of cobbles, thought to be part of the old Roman road which ran from Paphos to Polis. I circled part of the village, passing by a water fountain and some derelict huts to where two cypress trees shielded a mosque. Its doors and windows were the usual Turkish green, but it was the first I had seen without a minaret.

The village houses were daubed in painted symbols and numbers which, in relation to all Turkish villages, is a system used by the government to catalogue properties rented out to Greek-Cypriot refugees. Without too much renovation, some of them certainly appeared habitable, yet I discovered that only two families remained in Terra.

Down in the meadow, children were playing with a collie dog which suddenly decided to charge towards me. Having once bred these beautiful animals myself, I was somewhat surprised to find them here. Long grass and spiny scrub land is not an ideal playground for a collie, but its sable and white coat was in prime condition. Healthy and well groomed, he sat obediently as I stroked him. The children were so intrigued and delighted to see their robust pet sitting perfectly still, that they ushered me across the road to meet their parents.

Before I left the village of Terra, I was presented with a donation of thirty pounds from its two surviving families. It was not for me to compare, but their generous gift exceeded that of a major village like Geroskipos.

Mainly due to our previous day's struggles in the mud, my left knee had swollen again. After almost six hours on the road it was bad enough to call a halt. Where my surroundings closed in and the track became dense with maquis and carob trees, I off loaded my pack and applied a bandage. I rested, undecided whether to stay in relative shelter or risk a storm blowing in from the sea. Ahead of me were two more Turkish settlements, Karamoullidhes and Chrysochou, which bordered the main Polis to Paphos highway. I carried on, hoping to beat the rain I could see falling in sheets over Polis. The track emerged into open country to where a cornfield overlooked Karamalloudes, but the descent was too steep. With barely seconds to spare I found cover in Chrysochou.

Despite wearing a sweater it seemed a cold building. I heard voices, and suddenly two men appeared carrying the carcass of a sheep. They gave me a quizzical look, and offering them my best Cypriot shrug I pointed to the rain bouncing off the roadway. They smiled in agreement before hanging up the sheep and skinning it with large curved knives. I soon realized my shelter was a small abattoir.

The men were experts; not so ambitious, perhaps, as the vase painters that once lived in Chrysochou, but nonetheless, they were skilled at their work. The artists had portrayed musicians and horse riders as well as complicated ritual scenes, said to be inspired by the festivals at Aphrodite's temple. A Roman milestone was also discovered here, and now lies in a museum at Paphos.

The rainstorm lasted for almost an hour before drifting southwards. I followed its path along the main highway, crossing over the Stavrou tis Psokas river to find myself climbing again into the outskirts of Goudi. More fragments of history had been found here in the form of pottery decorated with illustrations of wild animals, which closely resembled a Rhodian vase-painting style of the late seventh century B.C.

This was a small Greek settlement, but I was particularly attracted by a rather grand property built on a ridge. It held two splendidly built stone houses which were separated by a large crazy-paved courtyard. It was a pleasant surprise to discover that later on I would be sleeping in one of them. Distant thunder mumbled its farewell as I left the village. Spring was turning to summer, and rain might never fall again on the island until next year. Come tomorrow, clear blue skies would encourage the sun to resume its unmerciful journey.

I arrived in Choli in time to see a lady appear from its church. At last, if fortune smiled, I may be allowed inside. The Byzantine church of Archangel Michael was without electricity. My guide, however, ushered me inside... smiling and bowing in her genteel manner at the pleasure of my company. I featured a scruffy tramp - but felt like royalty... such is the Cypriot way of kindness.

She lit a slender candle, beckoning me to follow her to the south vault where a contemporary painting of the Crucifixion adorned its wall. Without a word, she waved her hand around as if to say that once upon a time the whole church was decorated in them. As with every Orthodox church, several icons were prominently displayed, some lying end to end on a shelf above the pews. I studied them and marvelled at their structure.

I had learned that the resilient quality of wood found in the forests of Cyprus was far superior to that used in Greece and Russia, whose icon panels tended to warp. A technique used in the Byzantine period was to first cover the panel with canvas, then a reinforcing layer of gesso before painting. A method which originated in the mummy painting of Egypt. It survived throughout the Christian era and was adopted in the eleventh century by the Orthodox world. My only clue to determine Cypriot icon-painting is my sparse knowledge that a presence of turquoise blue suggests oils of a western influence - as this is not a Byzantine colour.

But its construction means little to the believer. To them, an icon is not merely a portrait - it personifies the saint as a divinity through which a worshipper can gaze into paradise. They are blessed with a heavenly light, and most, created in a time when medicine seldom healed the sick, became legendary for their miracles. The island must possess a saint for every physical and mental ailment known to man.

The original tower of the church was thought to be three storeys high, and used as one of a series of observation points in the reign of James11. But to me, a layman, it was just an interesting peep into a history I knew little about: a culture that could never be appreciated by merely passing through. But we are all committed to time and schedules; every minute of every day is a predetermined pattern of life's cycle... even to my friends the swallows.

The old lady had left me admiring the church outside, and with a beguiling grace these fragile birds swirled around the bell tower. Their lives are a never-ending journey. It is estimated by British experts that every year these extraordinary birds - with their migration from England to South Africa, constant feeding and nest-building trips - fly an amazing three hundred and five thousand kilometres. If a swallow survives for just ten years, its tiny wings will carry it on a distance equivalent to flying to the moon and back four times.

From Choli, the road wandered needlessly in several directions before finally reaching the older houses of Skoulli and the main highway beyond. I discovered the *mukhtar* of Skoulli was Leondios Demetriades, who also ran the exhibition of reptiles for the Herpetological Society of Cyprus. Both he and his wife, Eftychia, continue the work of Snake George in offering advice in helping to conserve and protect the island's endangered species. They try extremely hard, as Snake George did, to allay the fears people have about snakes. But seeing a viper on my first day in the wilds is little comfort to any walker.

Apart from the live exhibits of most reptiles found in Cyprus, there were two other poisonous snakes on view:

My friendly quide at Choli

the Montpelliar and the Cat Snake. From what I understood, both species have difficulty in biting humans... but seeing them from the safety of their display cabinets was sufficient for me. It was an extremely interesting exhibition, however, and I did actually handle two non-poisonous snakes, but it is a difficult and extremely dangerous indulgence to assume you can recognize these friendly snakes in the wild. It was always in my mind when walking to leave all snakes well alone!

Apparently, I had just missed Phylactis and a party of friends, who were now awaiting my arrival up ahead at the Green Valley restaurant. I spent an enjoyable few hours with Charalambos and Christoula, the owners, who insisted I join them that night for a wonderful family meal. Phylactis informed me that a doctor from the hospital had generously offered me the use of his empty house in Goudi. And later, well fed and watered, Charalambos took me back to the property I had admired earlier that morning. Inside was equally impressive.

The main part of the house was on a level with the courtyard, and contained a huge open-planned kitchen, dining room and lounge area with its traditional fireplace. Two steps up from the kitchen was a bedroom, and below this, stairs ran down to the lower level of the house. My first steps below ground were to the bathroom and a nice hot shower. The bed was firm and comfortable and I soon fell asleep, browsing over my maps. In the early hours, however, I was awoken by the constant yapping of two small dogs.

A Cypriot proverb says that if many dogs bark in the night there will come an earthquake. Where had these dogs been? Didn't they know the tremors had passed? I tossed and turned... pillows over my head. They just barked on, and whimpered until six in the morning... then silence. When I stepped outside to leave an hour later, they were curled up together outside the door fast asleep. I stood over them, wondering how so much noise could incessantly erupt from such a small animal? They looked cute. I nudged the nearest one with my boot and he opened his one eye as if to say: 'What's the big idea?... I'm sleeping!'

A wicked thought came to mind as I passed by a garden hose... but I left them in peace. An hour later I returned the key to Christoula, who insisted I stay for breakfast. She fussed over me, saying I was too thin and needed 'building up for the day's journey.' I had a good helping of bread and honey with coffee, while she tucked an assortment of fruit into my backpack. The morning news was on television and the weather forecast seemed ideal for walking: twenty degrees, with some cloud and light breezes. I set off at a steady pace, the family waving me out of sight.

In the immediate hills to my right was a group of old churches, the most unique of which, being Agia Ekaterini. This is a monastery church, marked 'Late Byzantine' on my map, once a large three-aisled structure built with seven domes. It is a dependency of Saint Catherine's monastery on Mount Sinai in Egypt. Sadly, its frescoes crumbled in the 1953 earthquake and only traces remain, but the church itself has been restored by the government's Department of Antiquities. It is believed that Saint Catherine was a Cypriot, raised in Alexander in the third century and martyred for her Christian faith. The angels carried her body to Mount Sinai where - in relation to another legend - Rigenna, fleeing to Egypt after jilting our rock- throwing hero, Digenis, built a second monastery.

There was a pleasant breeze climbing to Kato Akourdalia, but the clouds barely subdued the sun. A high ridge closed in to my right, and sitting under an almond tree I watched the ritual of two kestrels hovering over their breakfast. I ate an orange - seeing first one, then the other, suddenly fall like stones from the sky after their prey.

Almond blossom had fallen from the trees, but one could imagine how picturesque these two small villages would be in bloom: their white-washed houses; the nooks and sheltered hollows brimming with flowers and the smell of orange blossom; even the village names, Akourdalia, means 'wild garlic' in local dialect. And these pretty white flowers grow in abundance in the surrounding fields. Both villages occupied attractive sites, and had been part of the Laona Project. Kato - the lower one - has a folk art museum, and in Pano Akourdalia I passed by a renovated schoolhouse with its grounds now transformed into a herb garden.

It was a warm day, and although I had climbed for six or seven kilometres I felt no distress. Leaving the villages behind, I became aware of a strange calmness around me... like a hush that stills the air before a storm. Every sinew of nature had stopped its movement. For what seemed an infinite time - I was the only being on earth. The stillness was unreal... there existed an inexplicable aftermath of the earthquake. I passed through this strange phenomenon into a valley, where the silence was eventually broken by the sound of steel against rock.

Between crumbling stone walls I walked on to find the

village of Miliou in a mantle of trees. I came across two workmen. One shovelled dirt and stones from the roadway into a wheelbarrow, the other stood on a pile of rubble four metres high; the pick in his hands hacking away stone from an upstairs window. One house had collapsed against its neighbour. I shouted a greeting, and the bigger man leaned on his shovel wiping his brow.

'How are you my friend? What brings you to Miliou?' he smiled, his words a mixture of Greek and English.

'I'm on my way to Pegeia... Just passing through,' I replied.

The man was heavily built, his muscular frame more suited to wielding a pick, I thought, than a shovel. We shook hands and he introduced himself as Andreas. His workmate up above, paused long enough to acknowledge me, then continued his work.

'Things are very bad here and in Arodes,' Andreas began. 'People without water, electricity, or telephones. They live in houses which are broken and ready to fall down.' He shrugged his shoulders in genuine sadness. 'But what can we do with our bare hands?'

We sat together on some rocks at the side of the road and he continued to chastise the government for not acting quickly enough to ease the pain and suffering of the villagers affected by the earthquake. Across the street someone had tied a ribbon around a tree. Andreas confirmed my thoughts. 'That was the old couple's house. Did you hear they died?'

'Yes,' I said quietly. 'I was sorry to read about them. But

I never realized so many houses were destroyed. I saw the tents in Arodes.'

The word fired him up again. 'Tents?.. Ugh! ' he said in disgust. 'Tents are for walkers and goats. Not for people to live in!' Andreas laid a huge dusty hand on my arm in a firm grip. 'No offence, my friend. But look around you. Do you see any machines?.. Any bulldozers? Miliou should be full of workers!'

And every word was true. Andreas and his friend were the only two in the village. It was difficult to tell, but in this little corner alone, every house was damaged or destroyed. This had been a relatively minor earthquake compared with the one in 1953, but the inferior construction of some of these old village properties makes them particularly vulnerable. Nevertheless, seeing these vast piles of rubble was an unbelievable sight.

The old couple's house was a mound of concrete and limestone rocks. Fluted stumps of wooden roof beams protruded from the debris, and splintered bamboo lay among twisted metal. The solar heating panels and water tank had been crushed like paper cups. Even a sturdy wrought-iron balustrade, which had once formed a patio entrance to the house, had been uprooted and flung high into the branches of a tree. Still attached to it was an enormous concrete base.

Andreas tried to lighten the mood. 'So, you go to Pegeia? Then how do the English get so lost on such a small island?... Pegeia is through Kathikas. Back that way!' he laughed, pointing to where I had come from.

This I knew - but my route circled south and west in order to visit Theletra. So, not wishing to waste any more of his time by explaining my eccentric detour, I politely excused myself, saying that first I wanted to see the springs at the foot of the valley.

A natural and abundant supply of water to the village had created a lush green environment, and in spite of its scars and despair, Miliou was an enchanting place. Down in the valley I sat on a bridge listening to a choir of bird song and rippling water. The stream below linked with another, known as the 'Stream of the Fairies'.

A child might wonder why the magical powers of these fairies had not protected Miliou from such a disaster? A parent would try to reason... but no-one can determine the answer. Nature draws its own line of darkness and beauty, and at this idyllic place near the bridge I had now witnessed her two extremes.

CHAPTER 13

GUNS AND ROSES

In passing the old monastery of Agioi Anargyri, I had turned away from its medicinal waters and rheumatic cures, to climb a hill. Three kilometres from the stream, I wandered through the back streets of Giolou. It was a section of road I had travelled before, and the scene of conflict in 1958 when EOKA freedom fighters ambushed a British army convoy. But this time no-one waited for me; not even the pretty girl who had previously given me orange juice and sped away to find the *mukhtar*.

As I left the village, so a solitary man and his donkey arrived. The animal was barely visible beneath a pile of scrub, which was piled high into panniers and draped to the floor on all sides. It was not a heavy load, but amusing to see from a distance as it appeared as a walking hedge. It was a good opportunity to try out my camera which had been soaked in the storms. The man doffed his hat, and bid me good-day with a twirl of his white handlebar moustache.

I left the road near a tiny church and descended into a

deep valley. The sun burnt away my energy along a track which fell unshaded between the vineyards. A hundred pairs of empty windows stared down on me as I crossed a ravine; the deserted Greek village hung over the gorge like a frayed string of pearls waiting to snap and shed its houses. Where the road chiselled a horseshoe bend from the rock face, I rested on a second bridge. Tired and exhausted from the heat, I almost drained my flask in one.

Dating back to the fifteenth century, Theletra once had a population of around five hundred people. It was evacuated in the early 1980's due to the threat of landslides. A story exists, however, that the villagers had run out of land on which to build dowry houses for their children, and so fabricated the land slip theory to dupe the government. But the ruins of Theletra cannot lie: whole houses teeter on the brink, as if waiting in turn to disintegrate over the edge. Concrete floors overhang the road, and rotting balconies creak and moan even on the calmest of days.

I wandered around its streets, and near a leaning coffeeshop, entered the grounds of a church. Agios Ilias was built in 1775 and, as my notebook informed me, it held an elegantly carved *iconostasi*. Once painted in gold, blue and green, it contained a rare feature in the form of dolphins. But yet again, a church denied my entrance. I could only study its outer walls, where rendering crumbled like yellow icing from a birthday cake. Walking alone through these abandoned villages is to imagine the end of the world... to the old people of Theletra it probably was.

The new village was no more than two kilometres away,

Laden donkey at Giolou

but it seemed I would never reach it. Perhaps I had become too used to the comfort of cooler days, but climbing this steep ridge under a baking sun was soul-destroying. I found myself wandering from side to side instead of forward, my legs no longer a part of me. The panoramic views were some of the finest I had seen... but they held no meaning. My strongest asset to date had been determination and positive thought. These had now deserted me. There was no shade, and with the heat so intense I was simply melting.

When I finally arrived in 'new' Theletra I was so relieved that I squatted in the shade of a village house - unable to offer another step. I was now six hundred metres above sea-level. Tired, and dripping with perspiration, the village held little interest for me, its modern-type houses somehow lacked the character of old Theletra. I ate... or rather sucked dry my last orange, but it made no impression on my raging thirst. Then along came Theo.

I was dozing away when he nudged my boot, and with typical Cypriot friendship invited me into his house. His wife smiled at my entrance but sat in a rocking chair thereafter, her thoughts distant. I felt intrusive, particularly when Theo explained that the son of his wife's sister had recently died in a car accident. I offered my deepest condolences... yet there can be no comfort when a boy dies at the age of twenty-three.

There was little I could recall about the road to Kathikas, except the immensity of its vineyards. My thoughts remained with Theo's family and what seemed like the needless loss of life on the island's roads. Every year in Cyprus an average of twelve thousand accidents occur, affecting two per cent of its population. More than half of these are on the roads. In the past five years almost six hundred people have lost their lives; in theory, a figure that would wipe out every small village in the Akamas. Despite extensive road safety campaigns at the end of 1994, by March of this year fatalities had risen by twenty-one per cent.

Statistics show that the cause of two thirds of road accidents in Cyprus are due to excessive speed, driving too close to the vehicle in front and failing to comply with traffic signals and signs. In other words, elementary Highway Code regulations. Whilst the police, government and schools embark on a major educational programme for future road users, they overlook the glaring problems with today's drivers. Based on my own driving experiences in Cyprus over a two year period, I would imagine a high percentage of its drivers would fail a road-test in Britain. It has been twenty-two years since any revision of their Highway Code, and one need not be an expert to ascertain that driving tests are a sham. To read that twenty-seven motor-cyclists were killed in 1994 is shocking enough, but to also know that not one of them wore a crash helmet is a wanton waste of life.

Children continue to become orphans; whole families are destroyed. At the roadsides, crosses and shrines are tragic symbols of this increasing death rate. Youngsters, inexperienced and uneducated in the dangers of speed, will continue to perish unless the whole sphere of driving tests, tuition and legislation is not only drastically revised, but rigidly enforced by the police. Meanwhile, the powers that be should visit the cemeteries of Cyprus... they are rapidly becoming a resting place for the young as well as the old.

It was late afternoon when I reached Kathikas, and urgently in need of nourishment I stopped at a *cafenion* opposite the church. In checking the map I found that my route via Akoursos was still fourteen kilometres from Pegeia. I was way behind schedule.

The village tops a ridge of hills which run the length of the Akamas, and enjoys a relatively prosperous existence as a major supplier to the island's wine industry. Many vines growing today in countries that are world famous for their wine, are believed to have originated in areas like Kathikas, and introduced abroad by travellers during the crusades. According to one account, the high reputation of Cyprus wines was responsible for the island's capture by a Turkish sultan in 1571.

Curiously, I discovered the name of Kathikas listed with two very contradictory meanings: one after the Greek for 'perched on a hill' - the second, perched on something else... a 'chamber pot'! No-one at the coffee-shop supported either, and after also drawing a blank in locating their *mukhtar*, I headed south for Akoursos.

The surface underfoot changed from tarmac to concrete as I passed through the vineyards - and now on a hilltop, it turned into grey limestone dust. While the Troodos mountains faded into an early mist, there appeared a brightness ahead me as a sunlit sea cast its breakers at the shore. My track rimmed the edge of a deep gorge, and beyond, lay the still waters of Mavrokolymbos Dam.

Beneath the cliffs on a small plateau near Akoursos, is a legendary place of battle where two kings fought a duel to the death; it is called Laoni tou Tsakrii. On one side was the King of Inia, an evil and greedy man who was never satisfied with his own domain, so proceeded to conquer the surrounding villages. In opposition, was Rose-Petros, a peace-loving king who protested when his adversary encroached the borders of Akoursos. But rather than cause untold bloodshed between their people, Rose-Petros suggested the two kings should fight in single combat on the plateau.

After slaying the evil king, Rose-Petros hailed victory for his people, only to be shot in the back by a treacherous archer. So the gallant king died in saving Akoursos, and an oak tree - which still flourishes today - was planted on the spot where he fell. The two kings were buried in separate caves near the village. One is used by goats and sheep - the other, set in a sheer rock face south of the village, is the tomb of Rose-Petros... and is still respected to this day.

Akoursos teemed with goats: hundreds of them rummaged the hillsides, filled derelict buildings and roamed the streets. At the first house I spoke to a man tethering donkeys in a copse of trees. He shrugged his shoulders, neither understanding English or my prolonged attempts in Greek. My greeting to a second, much younger man, was met by a disparaging stare. He seemed annoyed as I peered into empty houses and began fussing a dog that came wagging his tail. He never spoke or gestured, yet I was aware of his eyes upon me throughout. It seemed obvious that both men were Turkish-Cypriots.

Perhaps it was pure coincidence, but nine days after passing through Akoursos a Turkish-Cypriot family was arrested by the Paphos police for possessing a cache of arms! A father and son were charged with illegal possession of firearms and ammunition, and a remand order issued for a third member of the family... arrested on suspicion of a murder committed two months previously.

The arms stockpile, some thought to date from before the Turkish invasion of 1974, consisted of boxes of TNT, several trap mechanisms, forty-nine detonators, six reels of fuse, magazines for automatic weapons, three shotgun butts, two Kalashnikovs, ten grenades, two automatics and three bags of bullets.

Newspaper reports suggested the police were examining a possibility of the family being linked with a Turkish Secret Service movement. And so - as with all what might have been's - these hypothetical questions later stirred my imagination. Why did the man at Akoursos treat me with so much suspicion? Could one, or even both men, have been involved? If I hadn't arrived so late that day would I not have explored the village more thoroughly? What if I had found the arms and ammunition? Unlikely as this may be, it's funny what you imagine. 'If' is one of the shortest, yet most thought-provoking words in anyone's language.

In contrast to this incident, it has to be said, that south of the Green Line Cyprus' crime figures are among the lowest anywhere in the world. Although crime has in fact increased over the past decade, its statistics remain imposing. During this period, whilst European countries averaged an increase of one thousand six hundred and forty serious crimes, per one hundred thousand people, Cyprus registered just one hundred and sixty. Its crime-rate currently runs between eighty and ninety per cent lower than Europe's. There can be no question that this figure would have reduced even further were it not for the crimes committed by non Greek-Cypriots. A prime example is drugs.

Because of its geographical position, there lies a constant threat from the narcotics trade. Southern Cyprus is relatively free of serious drug problems in the community; its only setback is in organized trans-national drug traffickers using the island as a stop over exchange from eastern providers to western consumers. Strong government measures, however, are seemingly moving the traders to northern Cyprus. But the north/south border is still a channel for prospective drug pedlars. Nevertheless, with their efficient crime-solving rate, no-one is more capable to combat such problems than the south. Their detection figures are extremely impressive, achieving over seventy-one per cent in 1994... while Europe's success approached only forty per cent.

On the southern fringes of Akoursos, new tarmac roads had been laid and a sign advertised the sale of land plots. Discounting goats and guns, this was at least a more convenient site to build, as opposed to extending the eyesores of hotels and properties along the coastline. Apart from Pegeia and Kissonerga, Akoursos is the nearest village to the region's most popular beaches at Coral Bay. Here, at the road junction to Pegeia, my journey to date had covered almost seven hundred kilometres. I was completely shattered. My feet dragged, and I was stationary every hundred... seventy... then fifty metres as I neared the village. I had been due in Pegeia at five o'clock, but when I finally saw Dorathy waving excitedly up ahead, night was falling. She and my reception party had been waiting two and a half hours.

It was a wonderful welcome, with people clapping and cheering as Dorathy came forward with Pambos, the *mukhtar* of Pegeia. He was a smart, typically business-like man, who vigorously shook my hand before making a little speech. 'May I welcome you on behalf of the whole municipality,' he said, kissing me on either cheek. 'We, the people of Pegeia, are here today to pay tribute to your courage and stamina... '

'What stamina?' I thought... 'I'm knackered!'

Pambos continued his praises, before handing me a bunch of roses: red, white, yellow and cream flowers, with their stems bound in silver paper... and just about as English as you can get. I was then overwhelmed by well-wishers, all eager to shake my hand. Someone removed my backpack, and I was spirited away and stationed at a table outside a coffee-shop in the square.

Meanwhile, Dorathy and the *mukhtar* had taken a carrier bag, collecting money from everywhere and everyone around the village. People continued to come up and shake my hand or wave from the street, and my table slowly filled with beer bottles... a supply that would have lasted me several days!

It is believed that Pegeia was founded by the Venetians, although some contend it to be of Byzantine origin. In his chronology of 1788, a principal church official, named Kyprianos, mentions the existence of the Zalakia monastery at Pegeia, this being one of sixteen monasteries in the region. A high quality mosaic floor was also excavated near the village. It composed of interlaced patterns of a variety of birds, fish and animals, such as lions and stags. But I would not benefit from seeing such treasures... I barely recall my head reaching the pillow that night.

My room at the Arizona tavern was most homely. I awoke to a perfect day for walking: little sun, the sky saturated in cloud, and a fair breeze rising from the sea. But I was ahead of schedule, so decided to while away the morning hours writing notes and admiring the ocean from a large covered terrace. The salty air and white-capped rollers pounding the shore, eventually lured me back to the sea. Free at last of my loaded pack, I winged my way towards Agios Georgios and found a track that led me to the Pegeia Sea Caves.

To explore these caves by boat is to witness a vibrancy of colour as the blues, purples and greens interchange with the water's reflection. Both sea and time have eroded the soft limestone rock into a series of arches and caves. It was a place where the Mediterranean monk seal used to be a common sight, the caves once being a peaceful breeding ground. Now they are rarely seen around the Akamas coast at all.

I walked along a headland where the wind and tides had sculptured almost life-like shapes out of the rocks in the sea. Tiny star-shaped flowers raised their heads from the sand, and in a distant bay a man sat at the water's edge. Upon my approach he stopped reeling in his fishing line to shake my hand. His name was Nicos.

He was a likeable fellow: tall and slight, with dark short-cropped hair. The fine bone structure of his face gave him a look of eternal youth; it was without lines, except for the faint crows feet at his eyes and a deep scar in the hollow of his right cheek. Only his hands, and the way he dressed gave away the years. His clothes were shabby, even for a man out fishing, and I adjudged him to be in his early fifties. Nicos was seventy-one. He laughed when

I asked him his secret.

He looked at me, mischievously. 'Secret? I have lots of secrets.' He cast out again, his old reel singing as the legered weight carried out his line. *'Kala!'* he nodded, satisfied with its landing spot. Nicos wedged the rod almost upright against a rock then removed a bag from his jacket pocket, from which he produced - like a rabbit from a hat - a small loaf of bread. He handed me a piece; it was surprisingly fresh, unlike the brittle texture Jim and I had seen rattling the table at the old-timer's house in Fasli.

We chewed on his bread for a while, then suddenly, as if we were in a crowded room, Nicos whispered: 'A glass of wine... working my land, and just being here by the sea... And,' he cleared his throat... 'sex every day! Maybe not so secret, eh?'

'In that order?' I asked. My serious tone and expression had him falling about in amusement.

'Ohi!.. No!' he laughed, holding his knees and rocking his feet off the sand. 'You English are so... How do you say... patti?...'

'Particular?' I offered.

'*Ne*... Patticlar!' He put his hand on my shoulder, but the look in his eyes told me I'd left it much too late to follow his disciplines. He explained them, anyway.

Nicos' grandparents had lived in Kilani, a village north-west of Limassol on the slopes of the Troodos mountains. Kilani and a neighbouring village, Pera Pedi, are said to have held the secret of longevity since the days of Aphrodite. Nicos said he believed that in these two villages today there must be twelve or more people over a hundred years old. He had my undivided attention!

'My grandfather would be up at five-thirty every morning to drink one glass of *zivania.* He then worked his land until noon. On his return from the fields he ate only bread, and a variety of vegetables and fruit before his siesta. Most days he returned to work in the mountain air until late.' Nicos paused, gazing at the waters lapping his feet as if he was there... back in his childhood. He smiled to himself. 'As far as I can remember he only ate meat one day a week. He came home at dusk, drank a glass of village wine, then he and my grandmother would go to bed and, er...'

He seemed too embarrassed to mention his grandparents making love, but I nodded my understanding. 'So, you exchange the mountain air for the sea, and follow everything else?'

He held up his hands in defence. 'It is difficult because Cypriots today enjoy eating meat. But yes, I try very hard.' For some reason he never mentioned sex or aphrodisiacs!

'Well, for all I know you might not be Nicos at all,' I reasoned. 'You could even be Adonis from up there in the Akamas forests.'

He rocked with laughter again. *'Ne! Ne!* And here I am wasting my time eating bread with an Englishman instead of fishing for Aphrodite!'

It had been a great pleasure meeting him. As I write these words I can still picture him standing there barefoot, his baggy trousers rolled up to his knees as he waved me off along the beach.

I had noticed fragments of pottery in the bay, some pieces of which would have formed the rims of sizeable jars. But none of this, the mosaic floors and the tombs in the cliff face below the church, was surprising, for in ancient times this whole area held a thriving Roman community. It was called Drepanum, meaning 'sickle', which referred to the cape.

A few hundred metres offshore I could see the small island of Geronisos, where the remains of Roman buildings had also been found in the excavations of 1992 and '94. I walked to the harbour and sat watching the boats, thinking about summers past and the romantic sunsets my wife and I had seen from the terraced restaurant above. But along this shoreline - as far as Cape Arnaouti and the Baths of Aphrodite - the threat of environmental damage has never been greater. As soon as development begins, so-called protected areas cease to exist. Even Lara Bay, one of the few breeding grounds left in the Mediterranean for the Green and Loggerhead Turtles, will lose its seclusion. The hatcheries will become as empty as the tombs I had come to visit.

I climbed the rock face, crouching low to enter a circular chamber about three metres in diameter, around which, six adult-sized tombs had been chiselled into its walls. A second chamber of rectangular shape was much larger, and contained six double-sized tombs and one single. The third, in which I could stand upright, was over two metres high and had perfectly carved semicircular arches above each tomb. These rock-cut burial grounds belong to a large variety found all over the Mediterranean, and this particular type has a long tradition in Cyprus dating back to the Bronze Age. In later periods the rock wall between these chambers was often cut through, so that one could pass from one chamber to another in a complex of rooms.

Shaft tombs can also be traced to this later period. Yet despite having a well constructed entrance of jambs and lintels, the tombs appeared to be without burial gifts, and seemed likely to be used only for slaves and the poor. In contrast, peristyle tombs were built in accordance to Greek Hellenistic houses, and as such, reserved for the rich and high-ranking officials of the community. Paphos held a prime example of these tombs, complete with Doric columns, in an area known as the Tomb of the Kings.

Agios Georgios is a popular place, with an early twentieth century church that commands superb cliff-top views. I passed by a strange building that the locals call the 'church for lovers'. No doubt a legend gives reason for this, but the hours had flown and there was no time to seek an answer. I left the sleepy harbour behind and headed back to the Arizona before darkness fell.

The tavern was very spacious, with extensive dining areas both inside and out on the terrace. Harris and his wife, Androula, had several rooms available for rent, all nicely furnished and with en-suite facilities. They were hoping for an increase in holiday bookings during the coming season, but tourism in Cyprus was experiencing a considerable downturn in visitors from the United Kingdom. This was partly due to high labour costs in the local hotel industry - one of the highest internationally - and the adverse effect of sterling weakening against the Cypriot pound. Although bookings from Germany and other European countries had increased, the performance of the UK market was extremely important to Cyprus, particularly to the apartment owners and businesses like the Arizona.

Next morning I sat outside on the terrace drinking orange juice as the family prepared to leave. By seven o'clock we were all on our separate ways. Androula taking Marianna to school, Harris and Georgios off to complete the pruning of his vines - and me, with energies restored, heading down towards two adjoining bays... one ancient, one distinctively modern.

CHAPTER 14

FAIRWAYS AND FRESCOES

A fair breeze was blowing in from the sea, but as Harris predicted, the day would become very much warmer. I was in familiar surroundings now, and apart from any foreign paths I might need between villages, my maps could be dispensed with. After a few kilometres I had turned back towards the sea in search of Paleokastron - Maa, a fortified settlement dating from around 1200 B.C. My track eventually sloped down to a bay where I began walking out onto a dog-legged peninsula. It was unbelievable, but even here modern villas were built virtually on top of the perimeter fence.

The ancient site itself was about four hundred metres by ninety, and lay some fifteen metres above the ocean. It was a peninsula that might have appeared easy enough to defend, but despite its fortified walls being up to four metres thick, flanking both land and seaward sides, the settlers from its first period were overpowered. They are thought to have been Greeks and Anatolians, and thick charcoal deposits lining the floors of the earlier houses is testimony to a ruthless end. These invaders were probably Achaeans, who brought with them a Mycenaean style of pottery which has been found here and on most of the Late Bronze Age sites in Cyprus. Excavations of the area, however, revealed a large quantity of sherds which have proved the promontory was used even earlier than this in the Chalcolithic period.

I walked between the square and rectangular stubs of houses, some with huge ashlar blocks like those of Aphrodite's temple, which had survived more than three thousand years. In one such building with a circular hearth, remnants of copper slag had been found on its concrete floor and a bronze knife discovered nearby, intimating the Achaeans use of metal processing. The Hellenisation of Cyprus began with the occupation and colonization of these Achaean Greeks. They spread their customs, religion and language, and secured the first city-kingdoms of Paphos, Kourion, Kition and Salamis.

Near this small peninsula was one of many beached areas that line the south and western coastline, all of which made ideal landing grounds and battle offensives for successive maritime powers. As if searching in vain for these ancient mariners, breezes constantly swirl around this headland. It was time to go; time for the wind to gather a handful of memories and return them to the sea.

At the cross-roads I turned towards Coral Bay, by-passing its beaches to find myself among gift shops, restaurants and tavernas. A major complex that has multiplied ten-fold over a few years into the region's most popular beach resort. On its far side, out on a rocky plateau overlooking the bay, I passed the entrance road to an exclusive housing project: a mixture of residential and holiday villas that saturate the headland. Further development was taking place up at the main road, with more shops, apartments and houses being constructed.

I noticed a sign: 'Under New Management', and realized how evocative it seemed. From the serenity of the region's mountains and forests, its hushed valleys and timeless villages, my journey had turned a full circle. I was back in a modern-day environment; into a glimpse of the future... a place, it seems, where Aphrodite will soon become a stranger.

The coast road ran for three kilometres before I turned away from the sea, and with traffic already brushing my shoulder I was thankful when I could walk along the beach. Along this open stretch of coastline the breezes freshen and rollers hit the shore on the warmest of days. Most times, too, fishermen are trying their luck with rod and line. But not today... my only acquaintances were a few herring gulls floating over the sea.

Although more than two hundred and fifty species of fish can be found in the waters around Cyprus, their actual volume is low. This is due to the poor content of nutrients, which have significantly reduced in the far eastern Mediterranean since the Assuan dam was built on the river Nile. A deficiency in plankton has resulted in a crystal-clear sea around most of the island's coastline, creating idyllic underwater visibility for divers. In a recent survey the cleanliness of its sea water also compared favourably with European Union standards.

The morning was heating up rapidly... a day for tearing off your clothes, running out and diving into these cool, inviting waves. I removed my boots and socks to test

Refreshing spring water

the water; it was perfect for me. I never had learned to swim - but what a paddle... brilliant!

Although basic similarities exist in the villages of Paphos, each has its own uniqueness, its mark of history and, to some extent, the key to its own destiny. Yet through archaeological discoveries, several of these coastal villages are unmistakably linked. The Chalcolithic sites found at Kissonerga and Lemba bear witness to their unity in an extensive area of settlements and cemeteries. These early inhabitants established an important culture, and a religion that worshipped a female goddess of fertility... a remote predecessor of Aphrodite.

There were five villages to see before sunset: Kissonerga, Lemba, Chlorakas, Anavargos and Mesa Chorio. All of which, stood within a few kilometres west and north of the principal town of Paphos. It was already approaching noon when I left the beach and crossed a stream whose waters had long ebbed away.

My route forked inland to where Kissonerga and Lemba lay perched on a hilltop. The former had a modern church which appeared as alien to its surroundings as I did. A lady sat side-saddle on her donkey while it drank from a spring, villagers smiled and waved, others stared in disbelief as I walked along the main street. Chairs were lined up in the shade of a coffee-shop, and a shout of 'English?' came from a solitary man wearing the traditional Cypriot trousers - *vraka*. I waved, and he tossed a twenty cent coin onto a tray, inviting me to drink with him.

Greek coffee, orangeade, lemonade, 7-up, Coca-Cola, amongst others, was always twenty cents at the coffee-shops. And from one village to the next, sitting with these complete strangers I could hardly remember when I had last paid for anything! A chorus of protest would ring out whenever I put money down to buy anyone a drink. To them, I was a guest... and I had learned that it was more gracious to receive, more important for them to give. No matter how poor, whatever these wonderful Paphians have they want to share it with you. From bread as hard as stone, to the most exquisite Cypriot cuisine, I had tasted them all... and welcomed them equally. My fizzy orangeade was no exception.

The old man was casting a disapproving eye over my boots. 'You need leather. Look here,' he said, lifting his foot in my face, 'mine are from Limassol. Strong... Very good, eh?'

I beat him to the punch line. 'How much did they cost?'

For a second he looked uneasy. Then we both laughed together as he realized I'd taken his next question right out of his mouth.

Spyros knew all about the Chalcolithic sites in Kissonerga - even naming them as Mosfilia, and further north, Mylouthkia. 'They found houses - but not like these,' he said, with a quick dismissal of his hand. 'Round, they were, some ten metres or more across.' He thought for a moment or two, removing his cap to wipe his bald head. 'There'll be no more rain.' he grumbled to himself. Then to me he said, 'Bones... and painted things. You know... figures and pottery. They found big cemeteries somewhere else.' He glanced at me to see if I was still interested. 'In another place. Do you understand?' he smiled.

I assured him I did, because this was true of the Chalcolithic period. Their burial grounds were outside the settlements, whereas the Neolithic custom was to bury the dead within.

My acquaintance spoke of the other site at Lemba. He scratched his ear. 'I forget what they called it... But they have the same houses and things. Long ago maybe this was all...' He suddenly changed course again, clamping a bony hand on my shoulder. 'Now then, my friend, if you're wanting the *mukhtar*, he's there... *Dexia*.' He pointed to the right with his cane. This was a belated answer to the question I had asked him when we first met. But it was a timely reply, for after leaving my companion I caught up with the *mukhtar* just before his office closed for the afternoon.

He was a kindly man, yet surprisingly, the only one I could recall asking me to sign a receipt in exchange for their donation. I was, of course, keeping careful records of all payments, and most times the *mukhtars* would check my 'accounts book' before writing in their own village's contribution. This sometimes worked to our advantage. In the coffee-shops they would make comparisons with one village or another and a few extra pounds would suddenly appear to give a friendly but competitive edge.

In the third millennium B.C. a site called Lakkous was the centre of this densely occupied spur of hills. Now its modern counterpart, the village of Lemba, was almost deserted; siesta time well in keeping with its villagers. The old site was south-west of Lemba, but being unfamiliar with its location I passed it by on my way to Chlorakas. Their Chalcolithic remains eluded me.

In November 1954 Colonel Grivas landed on the beaches near Chlorakas from the Greek mainland. It was from here that he began to lead EOKA guerrillas against the British forces. Forty years later my arrival from the north was not as stealthy. I was seen waving a white flag in the shape of a handkerchief mopping my brow. Jim, my Scots friend, was waiting in the square with the news that my visit had been duly noted by the villagers. Our charity had already received an official donation from Chlorakas, but there was an additional surprise. Jim's wife, Bett, had casually mentioned to a nearby building site foreman that I was attempting to walk the region's villages for charity. On wages day Thrasos had coaxed his workmen into a collection and later presented Bett with more than three hundred pounds. A magnificent effort, and the largest single donation of my entire journey.

Jim and I headed to the outskirts of Ktima, the upper town of Paphos, where he was to show me a short route through its back streets to the International School of Paphos. This was to be a meeting place on my final day's walk. Bett had kindly supplied fresh rolls and Mars bars, which Jim and I duly devoured whilst drinking coffee with the schoolteachers. It was a pleasant stay.

Alone again, I began to move northwards away from Paphos; the liquid refreshment I had taken soon turning into perspiration. Even in the earliest days of summer the quality of air in these lowland areas is poor. In the two kilometres to reach Anavargos I was soaking wet from the humidity. A road swept between silent houses into the older village beyond the church, before reaching a junction at the Vasilikou stream. Despite being so near to the main town, Anavargos was quietness itself. A few lizards scurried away underfoot and the head of a hooded crow turned, watching me from its rooftop perch.

Equally at home in villages or countryside, the crow is a resident in most European countries and one of the better known birds in Cyprus. The Corvidae, or members of the crow family, are reputed to be notorious thieves - especially where food is concerned. Their big brother, the raven, is particularly skilful in this respect. It's not unusual to see a pair of ravens playing tricks with an animal: one distracting it while the other swoops in to steal the food. Ravens have been known to follow hunters and fishermen for days, sensing that in time there will be food for them. The crow of Anavargos was not so hungry... but his black, staring eyes followed me out of sight.

South of Mesa Chorio stands the chapel of Agia Marina, which is yet another building attributed to local superstition. It says for a man to be reconciled with his nagging wife (that's if he wants to be, of course) he should gather dust from the chapel floor and secretly sprinkle it in his own house. I contemplated this upon entering the village... Surely he would be in even bigger trouble for making a mess?

After much to-ing and fro-ing I spent the night at the *mukhtar's* house, where Kyriakos and his charming wife ensured I ate until I could hardly move from their table. The following day was one I had looked forward to for a long time. I was going home. Not in the sense of completing my journey and returning to England... but home to Koili, the village I had once chosen to live. Yet it was also to prove a day of disappointment.

Mesogi was my first point of call, just one kilometre away.

It seemed quite a large village, with a typical mixture of old Cypriot houses occupying the central sector, and expensive villas on its southern fringes. The streets were empty until I reached the square, where pick-up trucks littered the pavements and a crescendo of voices erupted from the coffee-shops. After two unsuccessful attempts to find the *mukhtar's* house I continued west down to a cross-roads and onward to my next village.

My brief stay in Trimithousa began well enough, meeting a priest in the village centre. He told me the *mukhtar* would be there in a little while. The priest knew of my journey. 'Praise be for your efforts,' he smiled, shaking my hand. 'Come and join me. A small consolation, I know, but allow me to buy your coffee.'

We sat chatting in the coffee-shop for half an hour, and he talked of his early struggles working the land; of his decision to join the priesthood, and how he had later returned to Trimithousa to take over his own village church. As he spoke a man entered the room, sitting at an empty table away from us and the three other occupants. He acknowledged no-one, nor they him... not even the priest.

He seemed a strange character, and obviously not a popular one, so I was amazed by the priest's remarks when the man left: 'There's the fellow you need, my friend... our village *mukhtar*. His office will be opening now if you want to see him.' I thanked him, and wishing everyone good-day, crossed the street to a most unpleasant encounter.

At first I thought I had caught him on a bad day, but it soon became clear that rudeness was his bench-mark.

My polite introduction received nothing more than a withering glance. No!.. He had not heard of the charity, or my walk. No!.. He had not received a letter from his District Officer - and from the shambles of strewn paperwork in his office I doubted if anything was being actioned - and No!.. He was not interested in seeing a copy, or even the book showing proof of every other village's donations.

I was taken aback, to say the least. In more than one hundred villages this was the only refusal of help I had encountered. This in itself was disappointing, but I was angered by the man's dismissive and ignorant nature. I left him with a few choice words to think on... and his door almost came off its hinges as I closed it after me rather firmly.

Because of the open landscape it was a tiring round trip to the monastery of Agios Neophytos. But at the end of ten kilometres I could at least rest on my return to Trimithousa and enjoy some refreshment at 'Terry's taverna'. I had visited the monastery a few years earlier, but approaching it on foot one can appreciate - just as Neophytos did in 1159 - the splendour and tranquillity of its surroundings. Set in a sheltered valley beneath Melissovounos Hill, the area abounds in pine and cypress trees, together with the olive and carob that create a green and fertile valley.

A majestic church within the monastery is especially interesting, and contains among other treasures the sacred skull of Neophytos himself. But my sole intention that morning was to see the wonderful frescoes of the Holy Cave. I left my backpack below, and climbed a stairway up to the entrance.

At the age of eighteen Neophytos had left his home in a small Larnaca village to pursue his love of Christ and the Church. His search for an aesthetic life in other lands, however, was fruitless, and he returned to Cyprus seven years later to establish his dream. Now, as I entered the nave of his tiny sanctuary, it seemed beyond belief that more than eight hundred years ago a young recluse had carved out these picturesque caves with his own hands. It took him a year to dig a habitable existence.

A self-educated man, Neophytos became famous over the next decade for his teachings and Christian faith. So much so, that pilgrims from all over the island came to visit him. But with his privacy and monastic duties greatly disturbed, he dug out a second cavern, an upper Encleistra he called New Zion. It was here that the saint found solitude and peace within. He could follow services through a hole in the chapel roof and descend on Sundays to counsel his Holy congregation. Upon his return, he secured the precarious route after him by retrieving his ladder.

When Neophytos ascended - so to speak - to his refuge, it was a time that coincided with the decorative paintings of his original cave by Theodoros Apseudes in 1185. The frescoes are a unique collection, representing Jesus' life and various biblical scenes. On the west wall of the nave I met with a glazed stare from each of its twelve saints. All but three held crosses, their black robes, bearded faces and furrowed brows expressing a gaunt, yet holy austerity. On the opposite wall stood more sombre figures, with the saints Constantine and Helen wearing jewelled crowns and imperial robes, and a scene featuring the Ascension of Christ. This was a painting of deep feeling and expression, created by the simplicity of its authentic colours.

In the tiny sanctuary beyond, the frescoes held a softer appearance; the lines more delicate as though they represented another artist... another infinity. Overseeing these serene figures, the Almighty raised his hand in blessing. In his left hand he held a gospel. 'Come unto Me, all ye that labour and are heavy laden,' it reads... 'and I will give you rest.'

A small door led me to Saint Neophytos' cell where he had methodically prepared his own grave. The frescoes here depicted the Crucifiction and Resurrection, and were painted with beauty and compassion. But even more significant to me was the desk he had fashioned himself out of stone. For here, in this small cavity, he had written his life's work. Neophytos left posterity sixteen works of literature, among them the 'Ritual Ordinance' for monastic life. There are believed to be almost four and a half thousand hand written pages that now lie in museums and libraries scattered around the world.

I learned that a determined effort was being made by the present abbot of the monastery to publish Neophytos' collection of text. Its editing was to be undertaken by prominent Cypriot and Greek theologians, using pictures and microfilms of the writings. It is understood that besides its theological value, the writings of Neophytos will also reveal important historical information relating to the twelfth century in which he lived.

Saint Neophytos died in 1219 at the age of eighty-five. To rest your hand on his desk is to touch the coldness of stone, yet in the cell I felt a warmth... his serenity certainly remains.

A few cars had arrived at the monastery, and as I secured my pack a German couple enquired after the saint as though he were alive and well!

'Up there is the Encleistra... the caves where he lived,' I pointed. 'But his bones are back there in the big church.'

'Bones?' the man echoed.

'Yes,' I smiled. 'His skull is in there... You may kiss it if you want to.'

His girlfriend saw the funny side and began to giggle, while the young man tried to regain his composure. He was not amused. I made a quick exit out into the sun, looking back to see the German lass giving me a cheeky wave.

I walked back slowly to Trimithousa. At the taverna, Jean - an English lady - prepared me a Greek salad big enough for two. She vented her misgivings over the *mukhtar*, intimating that she would see if her husband might do something to help. I told her not to worry, but the next morning Terry took the trouble to visit me in Koili to apologize. Suffice to say, Doctor Phylactis was not impressed with Trimithousa.

It was two o'clock when I began the final uphill trek of my journey. A gradient that rose four hundred metres over five kilometres, along one of the most treacherous highways in Paphos. When the region's grapes are harvested in late summer this stretch of road is choked with a slow-moving convoy of lorries transporting crops down to the wineries. Tsada to Mesogi is a steep descent with hazardous bends, and no-one who wants to see their next birthday should be climbing it. To constantly side-step low flying traffic is not good for the heart - mine seemed to stop several times - so finding a track that veered away to my next village was a great relief.

Tsada's main church towers over the square and its coffee-shops, which by now lay relatively quiet. It seemed a thriving village, its narrow winding streets crammed with an assortment of old stone houses, modern dwellings and several derelict buildings under renovation. Tsada is rich in vineyards, with surrounding areas that stretch to the borders of Letimbou, Koili, Mesogi and out to the monastery of Stavros tis Mythas. This was a place I had visited on two occasions in order to write an article for a local newspaper. The monastery itself had once been residence to the bishops of Paphos, but its vineyards, fruit orchards, olive and walnut trees were now converted into the island's first major eighteen-hole golf course. My constructive criticism of its design, however, was not well received.

By courtesy of the Tsada Golf Club I had walked its fairways several months prior to the official opening. There was no question that its picturesque setting was perfect for any golf course, but seeing it from a players angle I felt that even after it had matured, its present design would pose few problems for even the mid-handicapped golfer. True, some of the fairways were narrow and not visible from the tee - and many required tee-shots to carry rough ground - but this wasn't testing for a player of average ability.

All the par three's on the course were straight forward iron shots, each having large 'target' greens. In fact, most greens were too flat and accommodating, with insufficient slopes or undulations. The one real exception being the thirteenth, where an elevated green had been constructed in three tiers, making it much trickier to negotiate.

My reservations were aimed at its much hyped-up claims of being described as a 'championship' course. In its present design it was anything but... However, there were a few excellent holes, with my particular favourite being the seventeenth. A par five, some five hundred and thirty metres long, which was full of essential features. Mature trees flanked either side of a fairway that both undulated and sloped right to left. With a stream set to trap the tee-shot, it again crossed the fairway at two further points near a green protected by two sand bunkers. Along the way, a hazardous bank swept down to yet another watery grave on the players left... a truly challenging hole.

This degree of difficulty represented less than a third of the course, with the remainder being fundamental tee-to-green golf and little in between to cause concern. There were no fairway bunkers or sand traps behind the greens, and considering the natural contours of the landscape, it was disappointing to see so many flat, uninteresting greens. I wrote at the time that I thought a professional golfer would comfortably score in the low sixties... which hardly makes Tsada a golf course of championship quality.

At the gates of Tsada's primary school I spoke with one of its teachers. A friendly lady who informed me the school was indeed a popular one, with a total of sixty children attending - fifteen of whom, came by bus from Koili village. For me, this was a little more than a three kilometre walk.

When at last I reached the heights of Koili, my penultimate day was almost done. The sun was sinking into a placid sea, colouring the sky and western hills in pastel shades that artists can only dream of. My wife would have arrived from England now, and I could picture her sitting out on the terrace of our cottage. She would be watching these same colours of light flicker and die in the valley.

CHAPTER 15

THE COTTAGE

Walking down to the village that evening gave me the same exhilarating feeling I had always experienced. The panorama that unfolds with every step is one of the most beautiful in Paphos. Koili holds an abundance of scenic beauty, yet although situated barely twelve kilometres from Ktima (Paphos town), it is hardly noticed by tourists as they journey towards Polis and Chrysochou Bay. Situated at six hundred and forty metres above sea level, it enjoys a cool and refreshing climate. Some three years before I had chosen Koili as my ideal place to buy a house.

Mainly due to ill health, I had taken early retirement and arrived in Cyprus in the summer of 1992. Having been on holiday to the island several times I knew its climate suitably eased my bronchial problems, and so, after initially renting a property in Kouklia, I began my search for a house. I spent hours visiting property agents, and weeks touring the villages around Paphos. With inadequate finance, my options were limited to either a small apartment or perhaps buying a derelict house for renovation.

It was by chance that one morning I should be passing Christos' office. He was a stocky, good looking man of friendly disposition, and one of the real estate agents I had met before. This time, however, he had some interesting news. An old cottage had become available up in the hills. Would I like to see it?

The property was situated on the northern side of Koili overlooking a deep valley, beyond which, towered the western peaks of Tilliria and the Troodos mountains. It was a still and clear day, with the greenery of Paphos forest visible on the mountain slopes more than twenty kilometres away. I was immediately impressed. The cottage stood on a small plot but had great potential; it was an L-shaped building of good size, with solid stone walls and outside loo to match!

It was by far the most appealing property I had seen. Two inquiries remained: the inclusive purchasing and renovation price, and for me to reconnoitre the village. The latter was done soon afterwards when I returned next morning to be given a guided tour by a man who is still my good friend today, Yiannis Ioannides. At the time, Koili supported just basic facilities: one small supermarket, its church, a barber's shop and the inevitable coffee-shop, managed for the previous twenty-five years by Costas and Panayiota Kyriakou.

Near the top of its southern ridge was the village school. A splendid building, with stone pillars at its entrance and large interior rooms. Yiannis had his first appointment here as a teacher in 1958, educating children between the ages of six and twelve. He told me it was once a thriving and happy place, but standing there that day peering through dust-coated windows was to bear testimony to the exodus of its young people. Along with Yiannis, the school had retired; it was now merely a haven for nesting birds.

We ambled down the hill, along narrow streets that dipped and swerved like the flight path of a swallow. At the village's coffee-shop Yiannis introduced me to Papas Georgios Orphanou, who had preserved the faith at the church of Panagia Chryseleousa (the 'All-Holy Virgin blessed with Gold') since 1981. The building was reminiscent of many Greek Orthodox churches that stand as a focal point in Cypriot villages. A large cupola rose high above its central aisle, with the apse and nave being separated by the *iconostasi*. This screen, in keeping with the splendour of its church, was particularly attractive and displayed many icons of sacred personage. But I learned that Panagia Chryseleousa was no ordinary church. For in the earthquake of 1953 it had been completely destroyed - and the people of Koili had worked without financial reward to re-build it. Their enterprise lasted two years.

Yiannis told me that disaster had also struck the edge of Koili in 1974 during the Turkish invasion. Low flying jet aircraft screamed over the rooftops to target and destroy a telecommunications centre which was situated one kilometre south-west of the village. This centre had been an important link for Cyprus to its overseas allies.

Apart from a handful of villas on its outskirts, the village itself held stone-built houses and cottages, many of which dated back three centuries. The building stone was mostly quarried and cut by hand near the monastery of

Agios Neophytos, and then transported by donkey to Koili. One can imagine in that era the incredible endurance of man and beast hauling these rocks for several kilometres along steep mountain tracks. The enormity of this burden can be measured by the fact that masons required more than two thousand such stones to build a single-roomed dwelling of average size.

A few of these old properties had already been renovated into holiday homes, with one belonging to a family from Switzerland. Their numbers did nothing for Koili's population, however; four hundred residents was Yiannis' estimation, and half of those were retired citizens. Indeed, the over sixty-eight population in Cyprus numbers around sixty-eight thousand, more than half of whom are women. Two government decisions had recently favoured Cypriot women, both young and old.

A new pension was being paid for the first time to persons over sixty-eight, and the main beneficiaries would be housewives who had never been employed other than to run the home and raise a family. This closely followed the formal abolishment of the dowry system. A tradition maintained in Cyprus for the past two thousand years.

The dowry's philosophy was based on the idea that a man should receive property by way of compensation for providing for his wife during their marriage. It was, bluntly speaking, in recognition for the woman being his 'financial burden'. With the ever-increasing changes in society, and in particular the role of a modern-day working woman, the dowry system is now legally invalid. Yet even though a dowry will no longer be part of a marriage contract, traditions as old as this can never be outlawed.

It is a practice, I'm sure, that will be decided upon by the individuals concerned.

Koili was only serviced with an electricity and telephone supply in the seventies, and Yiannis had said that until recently the village still relied on its water supply from the Troodos mountains. Like its neighbouring villages, their main harvest came from the vines. In a good year Koili produced well in excess of one million kilo's of grapes, mainly for the wineries in Limassol. It was also a supplier of almonds, carob, olives and a small collection of citrus fruit, most of which being sold to the local markets in Paphos.

What I particularly liked about Koili was its limited access. Perched on a ridge two kilometres west of the main highway, its only route in by vehicle was on a road that looped back out again. On its southern outskirts a secondary road led down to Kamares, but this was well away from the village. And best of all was the secluded location of the cottage. Away from the main thoroughfare of the village, it had its own access - albeit no more than a track down to the vineyards - but with a magical scenery that changed with every passing hour. Even the village name, I was told, originated from this enormous chasm below the cottage. Koili was said to be taken from the Greek word 'koilada' - meaning valley.

I had returned to Kouklia, my mind buzzing with all these facts and the exciting prospect that I had at last found a second home. All that remained was the cost of creating it.

That night I drafted out a plan of the cottage from my rough sketches and measurements. Apart from adding a facing window to the smaller 'L' section, which I assumed would be a bedroom, I concentrated on designing the main body. This was sixteen metres long, and I divided it into a second bedroom, a bathroom and an open plan kitchen - lounge - dining area. The whole section had only one small window which I enlarged, adding an extra three apertures to considerably brighten its interior. These windows, however, were the only modifications to its exterior walls. My idea was to create a comfortable and spacious dwelling without extensive alterations and elaborate fittings. I needed to minimize costs.

This was achieved with the help of Petros, a friend I had made in Kouklia. He came to the cottage a few days later with an architect, and together we completed the design. These plans were submitted to Christos, he and I haggled a price, and work began... eventually.

I soon discovered in Cyprus that words such as 'immediately' - 'instantly' - 'promptly' - 'now'... are much too aggressive. If mentioned to workmen, for example, they are always interpreted as 'later' - *'avrio'*. But frustratingly, tomorrow never comes; more often than not... it's next week! So this is how progress stuttered along at the cottage from day one.

To make things even more laborious, the entrance lane below was too narrow for any reasonably sized vehicle to negotiate, therefore access had to be from the rear of the property. Our only available place being sixty metres away which was, in fact, the main street of the village. Upon delivery, all materials were off loaded here and then transported by hand down to the cottage. The route was no more than two metres at its widest point: an uneven pathway of stone and broken concrete that weaved its way down a steep gradient between cottages and derelict buildings.

If nothing else, Christos was determined to complete the new roof structures before the winter rains. The smaller part of the cottage would have a flat concrete section, and the main area a sloping roof with red terracotta tiles. But to manoeuvre equipment, beams and heavy roof boards down such a slope proved a delicate operation. With each board taking six men to carry, it meant sixteen slow and hazardous trips.

It was during our fourth descent, just as we had devised a system of navigation, that we were ambushed. Our strongest man - who took most of the weight - was Andreas, one of the villagers. He and Asaad, a Syrian, were leading the way when a herd of goats and three laden donkeys decided to charge past. As we were buffeted by these rampaging beasts, everyone gained momentum down the slope and Asaad collapsed under the extra weight thrust upon him. A resounding bang signalled the destruction of one expensive roof board, and remarkably, despite being butted several times, I was the only one to stay on my feet.

Up on the main street a crowd of inquisitive faces had gathered to witness our predicament. Their eyes bore no expression; no-one laughed or even smiled at the strewn bodies emerging from the debris. From this carnage erupted a mixture of Greek and Arabic obscenities as Andreas and Asaad appeared. The village priest stood within a polite distance, raising his hands in despair as Asaad, still cursing, aimed a kick at one of the goats. Then there was a stunned silence as the crowd parted and two old women, with long forked staffs tapping the ground, followed their flock. Asaad smiled benignly, giving a courteous bow, and the second lady smiled back... before cracking him on the shins with her stick. Everyone roared with laughter as the little Syrian yelped and began hopping around as though his trousers were on fire.

The whole afternoon was a punishing one, particularly for me. Foolishly, perhaps, I had entered into the spirit of the occasion, eagerly offering my services on that first day. But heavy physical work had long been neglected by my ageing muscles, and I spent the weekend soaking tired limbs and digging wood splinters from my hands. Still, I was happy, pleased that work had begun on the renovation.

I would travel from Kouklia two or three times a week to check on progress, and slowly but successfully the roof sections were completed in time. One of the most exhausting tasks was moving sand and cement. Each load was dumped in the street and Asaad would have to wheelbarrow it down the incline to keep the builders happy. With the exception of Asaad, their working days were short. As winter approached, a shower of rain would send the builders scurrying back to their respective villages... but not the Syrian. Asaad continued his lonely trek up and down this treacherous slope until the premature darkness of these rainy afternoons descended upon him and he could work no longer.

On one such day I came upon him in fits of laughter. He was sitting on his wheelbarrow - a battered old thing, with a buckled wheel that squeaked and groaned as he pushed it, and a rubber tyre which constantly deflated. Apparently, he had discovered that its noises had a profound affect on the village donkeys, and with tears rolling down his cheeks he proceeded to demonstrate his new-found amusement. Each time he pushed his wheelbarrow several donkeys, tethered nearby, made up a chorus of braying. If Asaad stopped so would the donkeys, and whenever he screeched forward again they immediately responded. Asaad used the wheelbarrow as if it were a conductor's baton, and the donkeys performed a symphonic pandemonium, the likes of which had never been heard in Koili before. It certainly helped to lighten every backbreaking load he moved, for each day as other donkeys passed by a whole new musical interlude would erupt. With a hundred of these animals around the village it became a regular event.

Asaad was a quiet and intelligent man, who had forsaken a long army career like his three brothers to spend several years in England gaining a degree in literature. On his return to Syria he discovered that its economy had worsened and teaching jobs were now impossible to find. Unhappy at the thought of leaving his wife and child again, he eventually gained a permit to become a labourer in Cyprus.

He had few clothes, and whenever he got soaked by the winter rains Asaad would have nothing warm to change into. One unusually cold day I arrived in Koili to find a light covering of snow. The builders had left, Asaad's wheelbarrow lay silent and there was no sign of the little man. I eventually found him huddled like a snowman in a dark corner of the cottage. He was completely exhausted and sat dithering in his wet clothes. Asaad jumped up when he saw me, afraid I was about to chastise him for not working. Instead, I gave him the bag of clothes I'd brought with me and insisted he change. My trousers were much too long but he rolled them up over his boots, put on a clean tee-shirt and a thick sweater... and I was his friend for life!

All forms of renovation dwindled to a standstill because of the rainstorms, yet I had to be thankful. At least the cottage interior would remain dry under its new roof, and the dividing walls for each room were in position. This was how my wife-to-be, Joanna, first saw the cottage. It was on the third day of December. I remember it well... for as we stood admiring the vast panorama around the valley I proposed to her. One year later on that same date we were married at Gretna Green on the borders of Scotland.

With Christos under obligation to complete a second property in the village, the following months proved frustrating. It was late March before any significant work resumed, and by this time I was looking to move out of Kouklia. Christos came to a temporary rescue by arranging for me to rent a cottage in Koili. This was jointly owned by two Swiss families, one of whom I spoke with and agreed a rental for two months. Joanna and I duly moved in, storing furniture and belongings into every conceivable space.

One night in early June, when Joanna had returned to England and I was peering between tea-chests at television, I thought I heard foreign voices at the door. A key entered the lock and I came face to face with a rather irate Swiss gentleman... the other owner! He stood aghast, each question aimed at me with his hand ferociously banging the table.

I tried to remain calm. 'Obviously there's been a slight misunderstanding, somewhere,' I said, apologetically. It was evidently the wrong thing to say. The man's eyes almost jumped from their sockets, while a tearful mother-in-law, seeing his temper boil, thankfully stepped between us. It took half an hour to explain that I had rented the place from his partner, so dates had been mixed up with their arrival... and yes, I would move out the next day. Thereafter, Christos found the family accommodation for the night, while I started packing.

Once again the builders stopped work. This time Georgios and Panicos spent the day as removal men, ferrying my belongings down the narrow lane on a pick-up truck, while Asaad and I off loaded them over a wall at the front entrance. We laboured to and fro for six hours. Everything except a bed was stockpiled into the smaller section of the cottage, then Asaad and I went back to clean the Swiss family's home.

By then, our property had seen a big transformation, thanks in part to an Englishman who also owned a house in the village. Roy helped a great deal with interior work, and soon, walls were plastered, water and electricity was connected, the whole floor area had been tiled, solar system fitted and carpenters were installing part of the kitchen and fitted wardrobes. One major problem existed... I moved in that Friday evening without any doors or windows.

It was more comfortable than the first night of my walk, lying on a bed of stones by the river, but sleep followed the same restless pattern. Weird noises lifted from the valley, filling the cottage with strange echoes: murmurings that would not be given a second thought in daylight hours... but alone in the blackness of night they evoke sinister meanings. Everything magnified into a

Thanasis of Koili village

crescendo, especially the sound of lizards scuttling across the bedroom floor.

As dawn broke with its chorus of bird song I received a visitor. A head suddenly poked through my bedroom window, and nosing around was a stray donkey. I managed to shoo him off, then turning over to try and sleep I heard the clip clop of his hooves... He was in the kitchen. I led him out again, securing his rope to an olive tree further down the lane. Walking back in my pyjamas I realized he was one of Asaad's 'choir'. The Syrian used to bring them scraps of food, and in all probability, the donkey was looking for him.

I spent the remainder of the day demolishing the outside loo, using the heavy stones to repair a section of wall behind the cottage. Regrettably, Asaad never returned to his donkeys. Over the weekend he received news that his wife had been taken ill and he returned to Syria. I never saw him again.

The hot summer days slipped by until finally I had doors, windows and shutters... and I could sleep again. Meanwhile, tonnes of soil, bamboo and debris that once formed the old roof, and diggings from a deep cesspit, blocked any access from the lane. My mornings were spent painting the cottage, then by late afternoon I would be shovelling away at this huge mound.

During these early times I made several friends in Koili. Some of the villagers would bring me eggs, goat's milk, fruit, almonds and so many grapes that I could hardly eat them. There was Yiannis and his wife, Evdokia; Andreas, our strong man; my neighbour, Socrates and Nikolas the poet; Costas, who worked in a Paphos hotel;

little Georgios, the village barber and our *mukhtar*, another Andreas. Then came two of the old timers: Thanasis who was ninety, and Michael at ninety-three, being the oldest man in Koili. I would sit with them in the afternoon shade wondering why, in such a fresh and healthy environment as Koili, so many were smokers?

But then, smoking is common in Cyprus, where cigarettes are cheap and consumption high. Statistics reveal that forty-seven per cent of its men smoke compared with only seven per cent of women. And whilst the average international intake of cigarettes per adult was said to be thirty-one per week... in Cyprus it is fifty-eight. Concern is paramount in the findings that one third of its doctors smoked, and worse, that ten per cent of schoolchildren have experimented with smoking at some stage. An alarming message which is self destructive to a Cypriot's general immunity to heart disease: a resistance that is strengthened in Mediterranean countries by their healthy diet.

Panayiota, at the coffee-shop, cooked prime examples. She and her husband, Costas, also seemed particularly fond of my presence, inviting me to join them for supper on several occasions. Panayiota made the most incredible moussaka-like dishes, complimented with ospria: beans, lentils, broad beans and chick peas which were boiled and dressed with olive oil and lemon. Her yoghurt was also scrumptious, and noticeably peculiar to that produced in Europe. Usually made from a mixture of sheep, goat and cow's milk, the Cypriot yoghurt is solid, similar to junket though thicker and much creamier. The acidity in the whey also makes it more digestible than fresh milk, which is an important consideration in a hot climate. Needless to say, there was very little waste for the chickens from Panayiota's table.

Given the trend of building activity in Cyprus, it is impossible to rule out further development in Koili. When the coastlines are engulfed in concrete, beautiful hilltop villages such as this will be targeted. Its southern and western slopes overlook the sea, and already a sprinkling of villas have appeared. I would imagine that within the next five years Koili will link up with the ever-growing complex of villas that form a unique mountainside project known as Kamares.

Perhaps I had been lucky enough to choose the perfect spot on Koili's northern slopes, for in the enormous valley north and east of the cottage lies most of the village's vineyards and fertile land. In time, however, when the old can no longer work, and the young inherit these hills and valleys... everything will have its price.

* * * *

A smell of lemon trees perfumed the air as I walked the ridge. Birds lay silent, and the colours of sunset faded as the sky began to fill with stars. When I reached the cottage I could see the lights of distant villages dancing like fireflies in the mountains. At last, this was home... now for a nice cup of tea.

CHAPTER 16

JOURNEY'S END

It was hard to realize when I awoke that this was it... my final day! A day of complete contrast; of starting late with an early finish. Breakfast at ten out on the terrace was a luxury. Joanna and I being joined by her mother Jean, and friend William, who was to record on video my journey's end at Kato Paphos.

The morning brought clear skies with a freshening breeze, and as I reached the small wrought-iron gates of Koili's cemetery, warm sunlight shone through the pines. I was heading south, downhill all the way, on a walk that would stretch no more than nineteen kilometres along good tarmac roads. I would have to pass through the villages of Tala and Emba before my rendezvous at two-thirty outside a school in Paphos town... but there was plenty of time. My pace was easy. In a sun much kinder than yesterday, I sauntered between these spiny hills seeing no horizon... just a sky and ocean that melted into one dazzling sapphire.

Roads began to converge and circle like a spider's web. I had reached Kamares, a unique project designed and built by the island's leading property developers, Leptos Estates. This was a prime location several kilometres away from the sea, and with its villas sited on a series of ledges carved from the hillsides, owners can enjoy magnificent views of the countryside and Paphos coastline.

The project had been singled out as one of the five best in the world by France's International Real Estate Federation. In 1993 Leptos was awarded the Prix d'Exellence for its Kamares development, recognizing the project as '... one that best embodies excellence in all real estate disciplines involved in its creation...' More than fifty countries and eighty professional organizations world-wide competed for what is described as the 'Oscar' of the real estate profession.

It is, without doubt, the most exclusive villa development in the whole of Cyprus. Constructed among four hills it forms a complete community of residential and holiday homes. Each villa has landscaped gardens and the hillsides abound with thousands of trees, plants and flowers. It is true that the infrastructure is a great achievement, with properties carefully sited and no more than two storey's high... but where and when, I asked myself, does it all end? My train of thought was broken by the roar of diggers and churning cement mixers. Then, above the noise, someone was shouting my name.

A man I recognized from Koili came running across to shake my hand. He then spoke with his work mates who downed pickaxes and shovels to send me on my way with a loud cheer and generous round of applause. It was a kind gesture, and one of many which had so often lifted my spirits when injury threatened defeat. I stopped to acknowledge them, waving my thanks before trooping on down the hill towards Tala.

In the village was a Late Byzantine church, Agia Ekaterini, and its west walls supposedly contained the remains of early frescoes. But my attention was taken by two remarkably different characters sitting outside a small taverna in the square. One emphatically English, the other a charmingly drunk Scotsman.

'Over here, laddie. Sit yerself doon. Have ye a wee rest, now,' said the man, patting an empty chair beside him.

Well, it all sounded that way, so I joined him. 'Thank you. I could do with a breather.'

A few empty bottles littered the table. I ordered two fresh beers. The upper-crust Englishman shot a glance over his bifocals then, without a word, continued reading The Times. At that moment he looked vaguely familiar... visions of Armou sprang to mind. My interest, however, was taken by the canny Scot who, winking broadly as I sat down, proceeded to tell me about his villa up in Kamares. The Englishman seemed unimpressed - but his ears were cocked, nonetheless.

Andy was on holiday from Edinburgh. 'Me and the wife love it here... Been coming to Paphos since 1980. That's why we bought the villa,' ... yet another wink. 'Aye... The beer's not bad, either.' We clinked glasses. 'Cheers!' he smiled, crookedly... 'And many of 'em!'

He looked a well groomed man: clean shaven, with thick brown hair and bushy eyebrows. But he was painfully thin; his face deeply lined, yet remarkably handsome when he smiled. His fingers were long and heavily nicotined, the knuckle joints swollen with arthritis. As he spoke he gestured with his left hand which permanently held a cigarette... it remained unlit. His smart check shirt hung loosely on his frame, and it was obvious from the pain in his eyes that he suffered illness. Andy was, no doubt, enjoying his life to the full.

Ten minutes later he noticed my backpack. 'Now then... Tell me what you're doing with this lot... and you're walking, too? Hang on with me, laddie. The wife will be along soon, and we'll give you a lift.'

I explained as briefly as possible my reasons for walking, and he was impressed. As I left he shook my hand warmly, then gave me a crisp five pound note from his wallet. The Englishman, still mute, burrowed deeper into his newspaper.

It was five kilometres of open road to my next village, a land dotted with carob and almond trees but little else. To my left lay the ruined church of Agios Georgios and further, my route crossed the Agriokalami river in two places; both were dry and barren. I approached Emba as the sky began to cloud over. There was no fear of rain, merely the comfort of passing shade. It was one-thirty and all was quiet.

The village had been continually inhabited since the twelfth century, and there was once a sugar plantation here which had declined - along with the Venetians - some four hundred years later. Together with Kouklia, Acheleia and Lemba, it was one of four plantations that made up the royal estates in Paphos. But nothing remained, my only visible link with history was a church dedicated to Panagia Chryseleousa. Built in the thirteenth century, it had two domes - each adorned with a small Roman marble column. My notes told me that to go inside was to see its frescoes ruined by a local dauber in 1886. I passed by; my time limited enough to let the whole village disappear behind me.

In early spring the fields around Emba are renowned for their masses of wild flowers. On its southern reaches - near yet another church of Saint George - the rocks are a profusion of cyclamen. But soon the land would be without colour, engulfed by the grey concrete buildings of Ktima... the bustling town of Paphos.

I arrived at the school ten minutes ahead of schedule, but already my family, friends, schoolteachers and children were at the gates to welcome me. Two police officers were also in waiting, ready to lead our procession by patrol car all the way down to the harbour at Kato Paphos. The headmaster gave a speech, and a Scot's piper - arranged by Jim - blasted us away on the bagpipes.

Teachers and children at the International School were themselves doing excellent work for the hospital's charity, arranging various fund raising events. And that afternoon they helped tremendously by waving collection boxes at pedestrians and shopkeepers along four kilometres of the main highway. Our police escort moved slowly ahead, frequently stopping the traffic... I had never been through so many red lights!

The modern town of Paphos is also known as Ktima, so named by the Lusignans who, knowing the vulnerability

Agios Antonios church - Kato Paphos

of its port, centralized the city by moving uphill to their 'domain'. This derived from the Greek word 'ktima', its name and location. It is known that during this period an exodus from harbour towns to more secure inland settlements occurred elsewhere on the island. In 1566 a German traveller observed that Ktima was more fertile and safer from Turks and pirates than the harbour area.

Doric and Ionic styles can be seen in the architecture of Ktima's civic buildings, many of which hold wonderful collections of Cypriot antiquities discovered in the Paphos area, dating from the Neolithic age to the present day. But there were none to be seen that afternoon, the police car veered away down the hill. I remember little of the crowded town or the stream of traffic crawling behind us. I was striding on, oblivious of my pace. It was much warmer now and teachers and children had started to wilt; two boys opting for a ride in the police car! I slowed at a cross-roads, watching the procession of coaches and hire cars heading west towards Coral Bay, and some, no doubt, to visit the 'Tombs of the Kings'.

The impressive appearance of these tombs and their Doric style architecture could be genuinely mistaken as regal. Used continually as burial grounds for rich and prominent figures during Hellenistic and Roman times, this huge necropolis had since been looted by travellers, with some of its peristyle tombs altered by medieval squatters. In 1977, however, their importance was recognized by the Cyprus Department of Antiquities and systematic excavations began. They are believed to be the only architectural monuments here still standing intact since the Roman period.

During these subterranean burials the more illustrious

dead were entombed with an array of magnificent gold and silver jewellery and coins. The most imposing tombs have a peristyle court which closely resemble those found in the Hellenistic city of Alexandria. Yet although these tombs derive from an Egyptian tradition, their architectural characteristics are purely Greek. Some elaborate examples have a central columned court in the Doric Order, with rooms grouped around it. Their entrances were also excavated, and revealed numerous *dromos* leading into the burial chambers.

Around 320 B.C. the harbour town of Paphos became the island's capital. A possible reason was, at this time the island's economy and its trading of ship timber in particular prospered, whereas Palaepaphos - the old city - had no direct access to the sea. In the Hellenistic and Roman periods this new harbour city was surrounded by a wall. It ran west from the castle, then followed the coastline north for a further fifteen hundred metres to its north-west gate, before moving east to Fabrika Hill. I was now entering this ancient city.

My first steps recalled the words of my friend, Georgios, the old custodian at Aphrodite's temple... 'To dig the earth in Paphos is to reveal the soul of Cyprus.' His words personify the incredible archaeological discoveries made within the walls of this ancient city, which began less than forty years ago when a farmer's plough scraped over a pattern of stone. This man unearthed a fragment of the most beautifully preserved mosaics in the eastern Mediterranean. A discovery that eventually led Paphos into the official UNESCO list of cultural and natural treasures of the world's heritage.

Our procession marched on to the sacred tree at Agia

Solomoni; its branches covered in strips of cloth left by visitors as votive offerings to cure disease. The catacombs near the tree are of Hellenistic origin, and were adapted in the twelfth century as a Christian chapel. But in A.D. 252 seven martyrs of Ephesus were taken at the command of Emperor Decius, and buried alive in the tombs. Almost two centuries later when the cave was re-opened, it is said that the martyrs were amazingly restored to life. Hence, the tombs alternative name... 'Chapel of the Seven Sleepers.'

In the back streets to my left lay several other ancient sites, including the remains of Lusignan and Turkish baths, some interesting churches and further east, a sanctuary of Apollo Hylates, which dated from the fourth century B.C. One of these churches, Agia Kyriaki, occupies an area of considerable excavation. The church itself is dwarfed by an earlier seven-aisled basilica and archbishropic palace, both destroyed during the Arab raids. Their vast foundations, which surround the existing church, contain fourth century floor mosaics and numerous columns, including the infamous 'Saint Paul's Pillar'. Legend suggests that the apostle was bound to this column and lashed. His visit to Paphos with Barnabas is recorded in the New Testament, and at this time he also converted the first official of the Roman Empire, Sergius Paulus, to the Christian faith.

Soon the traffic, people, shops and businesses intensified as I approached the sea. A chain of souvenir and clothes shops, restaurants, banks, travel and estate agents, opticians, banks and hotels stretched eastwards along a sea front that formed the nucleus of Kato Paphos. Above the streams of traffic and people a sound of bagpipes heralded my arrival. I was now within sight of my journey's end...

This ancient city near the sea had harboured ships since the days of Aphrodite. In the fifteenth and sixteenth centuries it became a haven for small vessels which loaded cargoes of cotton, fruit, sugar and tobacco. The port and its sunken breakwater was in keeping with so many of the illustrious discoveries in its vicinity. But even as I walked across its new pedestrian zone, controversy was brewing over the harbour's one million pound facelift. The half-completed complex of shops and restaurants may still be scrapped, and buildings reverted to their original state. I well remembered the old harbour, its charm and heritage now bulldozed away.

Directly behind its quay-side buildings lay the ruins of a fifth century basilica, dedicated to Panagia Limeniotissa (Our Lady of the Port). The building had three aisles and measured approximately fifty metres by twenty; it is said to be the burial place of the Danish crusader Eric the Good. The church, like so many others, was destroyed by the Arabs in the seventh century.

On the shoreline stood a medieval garrison. Said to be part of a Lusignan castle dating from 1391, it was demolished by the Venetians and a fort rebuilt by the Ottaman Turks when they captured Cyprus in the sixteenth century. After being used for storing salt by the British, it was then declared an ancient monument in 1935. Also of Lusignan origin was the nearby fortress of Saranta Kolones. From the diaries of travellers between the fourteenth and sixteenth centuries, it can be seen that the ruined castle was often mistaken for the remains of Aphrodite's temple. The castle's existence appeared to be short-lived, however, as it was destroyed by earth tremors in 1222. Many of its forty granite pillars came from a nearby public square or market place built by the Romans. A variety of Corinthian capitals and fragments of white marble illustrate features of their architecture.

My thoughts returned to my friend Georgios, and the many wonderful things he had told me about Kato Paphos. His knowledge of archaeology had always impressed me. He would explain in great detail that the most spectacular archaeological discoveries in Cyprus came from Roman times. Their villas, theatres, temples, public squares, baths and aqueducts, being testimony to how their architecture transformed the island's cities. And that in the time of Augustus the geographer, Strabo, recorded the ancient city of Nea Paphos as possessing a harbour and beautifully built sanctuaries. Perfect illustrations of which, now lay a few hundred metres from where we stood.

On the north-western side of Saranta Kolones archaeologists revealed the extensive foundations of a group of buildings. The Agora, or public place, formed a peristyle court that measured almost one hundred metres square. On its eastern side was a raised colonnade, and west of the Agora a Roman Odeon was built against the slope of the acropolis. All were linked by a passage or gallery to a sanctuary nearer the harbour which was dedicated to Asklepios, a hero and god of healing in Greek mythology, who was often portrayed bearing a staff entwined with a serpent.

Despite a series of earthquakes that wrecked the city in this Roman era, successive emperors resurrected its grandeur, as well as its name, to 'Augusta Claudia Flavia Paphos'. The most remarkable monuments of this ancient city, Georgios had said, were the superb mosaic floors of its private residences.

The first, erected in the late second century B.C., is known as the 'House of Dionysos' and covers an area of more than two thousand square metres. This building represents a prominent Roman atrium style house, normally attributed to wealthy noblemen. It had more than forty rooms grouped around a central court that featured an impluvium, or open garden pool.

Remains of other prodigious villas shared this locality, among them the 'House of Theseus' - noted for its fine marble statues, including statuettes of Aphrodite and Asklepios. But most revered of all are the vast mosaic floors; their qualities are unsurpassed in countries ruled by the Romans. Classical myths and legends are perfected in lifelike geometric tableaux. Apollo and Daphne, Dionysos and Icarios, Pyramos and Thisbe, Hippolytos and Phaedra, Neptune and Amymone are all portrayed in glorious proto-colour, and set among geometric patterns, inscriptions and leaping beasts.

From Georgios I learned that four basic materials appeared in the ancient mosaics of Cyprus: pebble, stone, glass and marble. The earliest technique found on the island was a pebble mosaic, dating back some three to four hundred years before Christ. It contained small, mostly black and white pebbles, and featured Scylla, a once beautiful girl turned into a sea-monster by a jealous rival. The mosaic was discovered near the House of Dionysos, barely a metre under the ground.

From the mid-Hellenistic period a more elaborate type of mosaic was created from tiny cubes of coloured stone, called tesserae. They were cut to a determined size and mostly used in lavish floor decorations. This was the most conventional form of mosaic used in ancient times. The technique of wall and ceiling mosaics rarely survived; those that did are of an opulence mainly found in religious buildings. These mosaics were made of glass fragments, and in early Christian times they appeared of particular brilliance when enhanced by the additional use of silver and gold tesserae.

Within their provinces the Romans had access to numerous marble quarries, and an 'opus sectile' mosaic technique began to flourish. This involved cutting and shaping thin sections of marble into geometric designs, and encrusting walls and floors in prestigious patterns and figures. It remained one of their most affluent forms of interior decoration.

The Roman population of this ancient city was said to exceed twenty-five thousand, and their influence resulted in more than three centuries of peace, culture and prosperity... it is a spectacular heritage.

There was a calm over the sea and no swell in its harboured waters; the boats were motionless, lying like discarded toys on blue rippled glass. And suddenly I was there... I had made it! So many people were milling around offering their congratulations: my family, my friends in the charity, doctors from the hospital, radio and television crews, schoolchildren and teachers... Then someone was calling for attention, and a television camera focused on Doctor Phylactis.

'We are here today to welcome and applaud one man's exceptional courage, stamina and generosity...' His opening words brought generous applause from the crowd, and the remainder of his speech gave me a sense of pride in the realization that our initial target would be surpassed when all outstanding pledges and donations were received. My reply was brief, and equally, I was grateful for everyone who had helped me achieve my goal; it had been an incredible experience, and a part of my life which I would never forget.

The surge of emotion I felt as I completed this journey was a strange mixture of relief and regret that held no perspective. Only now do I realize its meaning. A part of me is still searching the valleys and mountains of Aphrodite's realm. I know I shall always return...

CHAPTER 17

EPILOGUE

He sat alone in the shade; a traditional wooden-backed chair tucked under an armpit for support. He wore a dark suit over an open-necked shirt and thick blue sweater. In his right hand was a walking stick... on his feet a pair of slippers. The old man looked familiar, even though a hand cradled his face as he slept. This was the village of Galataria, and I had returned to keep a silent promise to the man sleeping under an olive tree.

Agathoklis stirred as I approached, but not wishing to wake him I turned to a path that led under the trees to the church of Panagia Galatarousa. In my mind's eye I saw again the candlelit procession; the four men holding aloft their scarlet robe, ablaze with flowers; a smell of lavender and roses at the church steps... and childrens' faces aglow with the wonders of that Easter service. Almost six months had passed by, and although this aura remained, the church itself was tarnished. The stonework had been daubed in white paint, and I despaired at entering the church, wishing to remember it as it was on that starlit night in April.

Agathoklis had gone when I returned to the street. I made my way to his house. The old blue gates still dragged on the floor, and the only change inside was a few bunches of grapes hanging from the vine. Across the courtyard Agathoklis had resumed his snooze, and beside him, Thaleia rinsed vegetables in the sink.

It was a pleasure to see their surprised faces. I was embraced by both of them like a long-lost son. Our conversation had not been a barrier when we first met, and sitting together now was though I'd never been away. But my visit was short, as I had arrived from England for a special occasion. I was due to meet their son Phylactis, and make a presentation to his hospital.

After receiving news from Cyprus that our piece of medical equipment was ready to be installed, I was surprised to discover that the monitor was quite common in the labour units of English hospitals. This, however, was the first cardiotocograph in Paphos. Its size resembled a video machine - but twice as thick - and my enquiries revealed that the cardiotocograph monitored important activities of both the mother and her unborn child. It registered ultra-sound of the baby's heartbeat, and measured its mother's contractions. Their results being produced on a graph. The equipment could also be used for essential diagnostic purposes, giving a bio-physical profile in high risk pregnancies.

The presentation itself was a quiet affair, with doctors and nurses from the Gynaecology Department extremely pleased and grateful that their much-needed machine was at last in situ. My short vacation, however, was not over.

Even though I had been welcomed by my neighbours in Koili and visited old friends in Kouklia, there was one place that lured me back.

It was early morning, and sunlight had barely touched the ocean when I returned to Petra tou Romiou. Once again I sat on that same worn out rock, watching the sea as it murmured in gentle ripples over the pebbled shore. My thoughts turned to the face of a young boy featured in a mosaic at the House of Dionysos. His name was Narcissus, and in legend his beauty is compared to that of Adonis. In death... both were transformed by the gods into flowers. But what became of Aphrodite? So beautiful was she, that upon presenting herself to the gods on Mount Olympus, they all wanted her for their wife. So did these gods make her immortal?

To journey alone in the splendour of the Paphos mountains; to see the sun awaken a field of wild flowers, or to walk into the bewitching silence of a moonlit valley... this is to find the answer. For you will feel a sense of infinity... an alluring touch that can only be from the hand of Aphrodite.

GLOSSARY OF GREEK WORDS

*a*vrio	tomorrow
Ag*i*a	Holy (female)
*A*gioi	Holy (plural)
*A*gios	Holy (male)
biz*e*lia	peas
cafen*i*on	coffee shop
dexi*a*	right
dr*o*mos	street
*ei*maste	we are
embr*i*ki	coffee pot
*e*xo	outside
*e*la	come
end*a*xi	ok
f*i*di	snake
fla*ou*nes	Easter cheese pastry
glik*o*s	sweet
hall*ou*mi	Cypriot cheese
h*e*ro pol*i*	pleased to meet you
iconost*a*si	Array of icons
kaim*a*ki	coffee froth
Kalim*e*ra sas	Goodmorning
Kal*o* tax*i*di	Good journey
k*a*to	down
kl*e*ftico	roast lamb
kleist*o*	closed
koup*e*pia	stuffed vine leaves
m*e*trios	medium sweet coffee
m*i*lo	apple
mukht*a*r	village mayor
n*e* / N*e*	yes
*o*hi	no
Panag*i*a	Virgin Mary
p*a*no	upper
Pap*a*s	Priest
pat*a*tes	potatoes
parakal*o*	please
perpatit*o*s	on foot
pol*i* kal*a*	very good
sign*o*mi	sorry
sk*e*tos	unsweetened coffee
soutz*ou*ko	traditional sweet
Stavr*o*s	Cross
str*ou*thos	sparrow
sik*o*ti	liver
t*a*vli	backgammon
vr*a*ka	traditional trousers
yiatr*o*s	doctor
yi*a* mas	cheers
zivan*i*a	alcoholic drink

oi reads *i*
ei reads *i*
ou reads *u*

Stress letters in *italic* when read, eg. *a*vrio

All Greek words that appear in the glossary are *italic* in book text

N
KHRYSOKHOU BAY.
Pomos Point
Pomos
Kato Gialia
Gialia
Baths of Aphrodite
Polis
Pelathousa
AKAMAS.
Fasli
Lyso
CYPRUS.
R. Ezousas
R. Xeros
Fyti
Gialou
Kathikos
Theletra
Kannaviou
Asprogia
Pano Panagia
Drepanum
Pegeia
Polemi
Galataria
Lemona
Koili
Coral Bay
Agios Ioannis
Arminou
Agios Nic
Pentalia
Mesana
Tala
Kissonerga
Mesogi
Lemba
Episkopi
Kelokedara
Kidasi
PAPHOS.
PAFOS
Geroskipos
Stavrokono
Prastio
Mousere
Kato Paphos
(Finish.)
Timi
Paphos International Airport
Mandria
Kouklia
Authors Route
Petra tou Romiou
(Start.)
SCALE 1: 50,000.